HOW MANY CHILDREN?

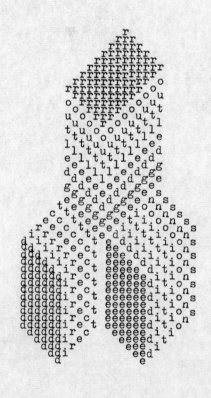

HOW MANY CHILDREN ?

ANN CARTWRIGHT
Institute for Social Studies in Medical Care

ROUTLEDGE DIRECT EDITIONS

ROUTLEDGE & KEGAN PAUL
London, Henley and Boston

First published in 1976
by Routledge & Kegan Paul Ltd
76 Carter Lane,
London EC4V 5EL and
Reading Road,
Henley-on-Thames
Oxon RG9 1EN and
9 Park Street,
Boston, Mass. 02108, USA
Manuscript typed by Betty R Ozzard
Printed and bound in Great Britain by
Unwin Brothers Limited,
The Gresham Press, Old Woking, Surrey
A member of the Staples Printing Group

ISBN 0 7100 8341 6

CONTENTS

    Intentions (p.165)   Economic influences (p.166)
    Family relationships (p.167)   Birth control (p.168)
    Dangers of current developments in birth control
    services and information (p.168)   Implications for
    the future (p.170)

Appendix I THE SAMPLE   172
    The study areas (p.172)   The sample of births (p.172)
    Comparison of some factual data from mothers and
    fathers (p.178)   The movers (p.178)

Appendix II CLASSIFICATION OF SOCIAL CLASS   180

Appendix III STATISTICAL SIGNIFICANCE AND SAMPLING ERRORS   183

Appendix IV FAMILY SIZE AND THE BIAS IN THE SAMPLE   186

    BIBLIOGRAPHY   188

    INDEX   192

ACKNOWLEDGMENTS

Many people have helped and contributed to this study:

The mothers and fathers who answered our questions.

The Office of Population Censuses and Surveys who financed the study, particularly Jean Thompson who initiated it, Amelia Harris who acted as liaison officer, and I. Hutchinson and D.M. Stobart who selected the sample.

The interviewers: Margery Thorne, Flo Green, Joan Cattell, Janet Martin, Sheila Chetham, Lilian Blaine, Auriol Gardner, Janet Parker, Carole Powell, Marion Thomas, Muriel Toney, Mollie Richards, Mair Hill, Ruth Foster, Hilary Gellman, Isobel Wiburg, Lyn Muller, Veronica Geal, Gwen Shaw, Carole Telfer, Connie Frost, Helen MacLennan, Jaclyn McAlister, Rosemary Rennie, Mavis Evans, Betty Renaudon, Dorothy Deave, Miriam Kleiner, Gaynor Lang, Margaret Bourne and others.

The coders: Jane Wadsworth, Margaret Hall, Phyl Jones, Gwen Cartwright, Jenny Broome, Tony Michael, Brian Nicholls, Margaret Anderson, Rosemary Jenkins, Quita Glynn and others.

The machine operators and punchers: Alison Britton, Joan Deane, Dorothy Hills and Ann Pentol.

Joanna Garcia worked on the pilot study and helped with the planning and organization of the field work. Elizabeth Prince designed and organized much of the coding and helped with analyses for the appendices. Warwick Wilkins checked and commented on the report.

Members of the Institute's Advisory Committee, Abe Adelstein, Leslie Best, Bill Brass, Vera Carstairs, John Fry, Geoffrey Hawthorn, Austin Heady (Chairman), Margot Jefferys, Joyce Leeson, John McEwan, Louis Moss, Alan Snaith, Gordon Trasler, Michael Warren helped at various stages.

Others who gave advice and help are Janet Askham, Margaret Bone, Del Carr, Henry Hardman, Christopher Langford, Kimmo Leppo, Peter Marris, David Pearce, John Simons, Alwyn Smith, Marjorie Waite and Peter Willmott.

Queen Mary College, University of London, let us use their machines.

People who helped in various other ways are Rene Alinson, Ashok Bhasin, Barbara Edwards, Christine Fitz-Gerald, Wyn Tucker and Michael Willmott.

Colleagues who gave constant encouragement and help are Janet Ball, Howard Dickinson, Christine Farrell, Leonie Kellaher, Sue Lucas and Maureen O'Brien.

I am grateful to them all.

AUTHOR'S NOTE

A copy of the questionnaire may be obtained from the Institute of Social Studies in Medical Care, 18 Victoria Park Square, London E2. There will be a charge for photocopying when supplies run out.

Chapter 1

INTRODUCTION

AIMS

This is a study of family size and family spacing in England and
Wales in 1973.   Basically it is about three things.   First, people's
intentions about family size and family spacing;   that is the extent
to which and stage at which people have firm intentions about their
family structure, and the nature of their intentions in terms of
sex composition, numbers, upper or lower limits and timing.
Secondly, the factors that are, or may be, related to people's
family intentions, or lack of intentions - their work, housing,
marital relationships and family roles, their economic situation
and their perceptions of these factors.   Thirdly, the influences
on people's achievement of, or failure to achieve, their intentions,
particularly their use of, and attitudes to, contraception, abortion
and birth control services.

In looking at these intentions and the factors related to them
and their achievement, a major interest is in changes over time.
The study attempts to throw some light on the falling birth rate
and the relative contributions of desires for smaller families,
different spacing patterns, and the use of more effective methods
of birth control.   Comparisons are made with an earlier study,
'Parents and Family Planning Services' (Cartwright, 1970), and,
like that study, this one is based on interviews with the mothers
and fathers of a random sample of legitimate births in England and
Wales.

There are a number of implications of this sample base.   One
obvious limitation is that there is no information about either
illegitimate births or couples with no children.   If the proportion
or pattern of illegitimate births is changing or if more couples are
postponing the birth of their first child or not having any children
at all, this would seriously affect the usefulness of the study.
The extent to which either of these is happening is looked at later
in this chapter.   Another complication is that by taking a sample
of births the sample is biased towards parents who will have
relatively large families.   This is illustrated by taking the
distribution of family size at the time of interview and on the
obviously unrealistic assumption that fertility remains constant

over time, calculating the final family size of the sample and the
population from which it was drawn. (Details of the calculation are
in Appendix IV.)   This shows that the average number of children
in the sample at the time of interview was 1.96, and that the sample
would have an average final family size of 2.93 children whereas the
completed family size of the population from which it was selected
would be 2.40 children.   But the individuals who will have a
particular number of children cannot be identified with any
certainty.   The sample cannot therefore be reweighted in any
straightforward way to correct for this bias.   It needs to be borne
in mind continuously when looking at the results.   However, many of
the analyses relate to comparisons of couples with different family
size expectations.   The bias should not affect such comparisons,
only the overall distribution.

    The sample has a number of advantages.   One is that by defining
the sample in this way a relatively high proportion of parents are
likely to respond and to have a feeling of involvement in the study.
People who have been selected because they have recently had a baby
seem to understand and accept the basis of selection better and to
identify with the survey more, because they have been chosen for a
clearly defined positive reason, than people chosen 'at random from
the list of voters'.   A practical advantage is that mothers of
young children are often at home much of the time so are relatively
easy to contact and often prepared to spend time being interviewed.

    But probably the most important advantage is that the interviews
took place soon after people must have made 'decisions' about
whether to have another baby soon after the last one, and what
method of contraception, if any, to use at that particular stage in
their lives.   These 'decisions' may have been taken after careful
deliberation or they may be negative ones in the sense that no
decision and no action was taken which has obvious implications for
likely future events.   Either way, parents of young babies will
have inevitably passed through a critical phase in their family
building programme.   They were seen soon after this crucial phase
and therefore at a relatively good time to explain and tell us
about the decision-making process (or lack of it) as they saw it.
Moreover, the decisions they were asked about were generally
perceived as important ones for them, so for the most part they
were interested and willing to discuss them.

    A final advantage was more pertinent to the earlier study than
to the present one.   Most mothers with young babies have had
recent contact with various health services: the majority have had
their baby in hospital, and they have nearly all been in touch with
their general practitioner and health visitor.   This enables the
study to look at the part played by different branches of the
health service in giving advice and help about contraception to
mothers around the time they have a baby.

    So although the study was based on a sample similar to the one
designed for another project with a different aim, there are a
number of reasons why such a sample may be particularly helpful in
illuminating the family building process, as long as the limitations
of the approach are clearly recognized.

METHODS

The study was done in 25 local authority areas in England and Wales
between March and August 1973: London boroughs, county boroughs,
municipal boroughs, urban districts or rural districts, or combin-
ations of such areas. (The way in which this was done and further
details about the sample are described in Appendix I.)   To choose
them, areas were stratified first by region and then, within region,
by county.   They were chosen with a probability proportional to
the number of births in 1970.   If a local authority had fewer than
350 births in 1970 it was combined with one or more near-by areas,
so that there were 350 or more births in 1970 in all our sample
areas.   A list of the study areas is contained in Appendix I. In
size they ranged from Birmingham with 18,141 births, to Welling-
borough R.D. in Northamptonshire with 378.   There were four London
boroughs, seven county boroughs, three entirely rural areas and
another three contained a rural district.   Geographically they
stretched from Plymouth to Berwick-upon-Tweed and from Maryport and
Workington to Rochester.
   Areas with a large number of births had a greater chance of
being included than areas with a small number.   Within each area
the Office of Population Censuses and Surveys selected a sample of
eighty legitimate births registered in the last quarter of 1972.
(Multiple births were treated as a single birth as the sample unit
was the mother or father not the baby.)   So in small areas each
birth had a relatively large chance of being selected, in large
ones a small chance.   The combination of the two chances for areas,
and for births within areas, meant that every legitimate birth in
England and Wales in the study period had an equal chance of being
included in the sample.   It is a statistically random sample of
legitimate births.
   Within each area 67 of the 80 births were allocated systematically to the sample of mothers, 13 to the sample of fathers.   This
means there are comparable samples of mothers and fathers - but a
much larger one of mothers.
   A letter was sent to each of the mothers and fathers selected
for the study. It was on our headed notepaper and said:
   The Institute for Social Studies in Medical Care is doing a
   study of families with young children in this area and may be
   asking for your help.   If one of our team calls on you we hope
   you will agree to be interviewed.
      All the information given to us will be treated with the
   strictest confidence and will not be passed to anyone outside
   the Institute.   We plan to write a book about the study but it
   will not be possible to identify the people taking part; no
   names will be mentioned in it.
      To do this study we have picked from the register of births
   a cross-section of people who have recently had a baby. We can
   only get a true picture if we are able to see all the people
   whose names have been chosen.
      You may like to know that the Institute for Social Studies in
   Medical Care is a non-profit research institute which has
   published a number of books about health services and how people
   use them.   Several doctors have helped in planning this study

and deciding what questions to ask.

Thank you, in advance, for your help.

In the earlier study we had found that the response from fathers was better when we sent them a letter about the study than when we did not, but the letter did not appear to make any difference to the response from mothers (Cartwright and Tucker, 1969).

Both mothers and fathers were interviewed by women interviewers. In a pilot study interviews with fathers were systematically divided between men and women interviewers (Cartwright and Moffet, 1974). There was no difference in the response rate of the two groups and although there were some differences in the types of answers given to certain questions, most of the differences might have occurred by chance.   We could not see any clear pattern in the sorts of response that varied, so did not feel it was necessary to recruit and train men to interview fathers on the main study.

Response

The overall response on the main study was 87%.   That for mothers was 88% and for fathers 81%.   This is shown in Table 1.

TABLE 1   Response from mothers and fathers

	Mothers		Fathers		Total	
	No.	%	No.	%	No.	%
Completed	1,473	88	263	81	1,736	87
Definite refusal	129	8	31	9	160	8
Other refusal	29	2	6	2	35	2
Not traced	23	1	6	2	29	1
Temporarily away	5	-	7	2	12	1
Other	-	-	2	1	2	-
Father - now separated*	-	-	5	1	5	-
Died	-	-	2	1	2	-
Left England and Wales	16	1	3	1	19	1
Total	1,675	100	325	100	2,000	100

* If a father was no longer living with the baby's mother, no attempt was made to interview him, but if a mother had separated from her husband she was still asked to co-operate.

The proportions cannot be compared directly with the response rates in 'Parents and Family Planning Services', as in that study no attempt was made to follow up parents who had left the study areas.   Of those still living in the study areas, 91% of the mothers and 82% of the fathers were interviewed on that study, that is 83% of the total sample of mothers, 71% of fathers.   In the present study the proportion of those interviewed who had moved out of the study areas was 2% of mothers, 5% of fathers. The inclusion of these small proportions is unlikely to affect comparisons between the two surveys.   This is demonstrated in

Appendix I where the characteristics of those who had moved are also described.

The interviews

Most of the interviews, two-thirds, took between an hour and an hour and a half.   Only 7% took less than an hour.   The husband was present for some of the time at 16% of the interviews with mothers, the wife for a much larger proportion, 77%, of the interviews with husbands.   This was in spite of attempts to interview the mother or father alone whenever possible.   In 'Parents and Family Planning Services' wives were present at 58% of the interviews with fathers. It may be that fathers are less willing to be interviewed on their own by women than by men interviewers.
       Most interviews, 92%, were carried out during March-June 1973. A few were done later.   The age of the baby at the time is shown in Table 2 for both the current study and for 'Parents and Family Planning Services'.

TABLE 2   Age of baby at time of interview

| | Current study | | | 'Parents and Family Planning Services' |
	Mothers	Fathers	Total	
	%	%	%	%
Baby died	2	1	2	1
Less than 4 months	2	1	2	-
4 months < 5 months	8	7	8	3
5 months < 6 months	27	19	25	21
6 months < 7 months	29	26	29	46
7 months < 8 months	20	26	21	21
8 months < 9 months	9	13	9	5
9 months or more	3	7	4	3
Number of mothers or fathers (= 100%)	1,473	263	1,736	1,752

       There was a longer interval between the baby's birth and interviews with fathers than with mothers.   This was probably because the fathers were more elusive.   Sixteen per cent of the interviews with fathers were done after June 1973 when the field work was supposed to end, 7% of the interviews with mothers.   Altogether the scatter is rather wider than that in 'Parents and Family Planning Services'.   Nine-tenths of the interviews in that survey were done when the baby was five to seven months old, compared with three-quarters in the present study.

Recalls

To check the repeatability of the basic data a random one in four of the mothers interviewed was called on again two - six months

after the initial interview.   They were seen by a different interviewer who had no knowledge of the earlier replies.   A number of
key questions were repeated and the mothers were also asked about
various changes since the previous interview.   The results showed
that the use of contraceptive methods involving an agent or
appliance was reported more consistently than the use of methods
such as withdrawal and the safe period.   The question on whether
they hoped for further children was answered in the same way on
both occasions by 88% of the mothers, 10% switched either to or
from being uncertain on one occasion, only 2% changed radically:
1% from 'yes' to 'no', 1% from 'no' to 'yes'.   (For further details
see Cartwright and Prince, 1975.)

But if mothers give the same answers to a question on two
occasions it does not necessarily mean that the answers are
accurate or that they reflect attitudes appropriately.   And different answers may reflect a genuine change in attitudes or circumstances.   Nevertheless a repeat survey gives some indications of
the limitations of the data and results from this study are used to
put various findings in perspective.

BACKGROUND TO THE STUDY

The demographic backcloth to this study was the recent dramatic
fall in the birth rate.   In 1964 the birth rate in England and
Wales (live births per 1,000 women aged 15-44) was higher, 93.0,
than it had been for fifty years (Office of Population Censuses
and Surveys, 1975).   Since then it has fallen, gradually at first,
to 84.3 in 1970 and 84.0 in 1971, then more dramatically to 77.5
in 1972 and 71.7 in 1973.   Hawthorn (1974) explained the peak in
1964 in this way:

> In the early sixties, women over 30 were either making up for
> postponed births or having ones they had not anticipated;   women
> in their late twenties were doing the same to a hitherto
> unmatched degree;   and women in their early twenties were having
> very early what look like being slightly smaller families than
> those of their immediate predecessors.

There seems to be general agreement about this interpretation.
Another expert put it like this:

> the major part of the rise in annual births...was a borrowing of
> births from the future due to earlier marriage and shorter
> intervals between marriage and first birth, and also between
> subsequent births.   The baby which might in previous conditions
> be born in 1960 three years after marriage which had occurred at
> age 26, was born in 1956 two years after a marriage which had
> occurred at age 23.   The downward trend in the frequency of
> births since 1964 (when this borrowing from the future has
> exhausted itself, as it had to) was first apparent among women
> in the older childbearing ages whose children were born
> relatively early in marriage ('New Society', 1975).

Among women aged 15-19 the peak in the birth rate was some years
later.   It went on rising from 42.7 in 1964 to 51.0 in 1971 but
fell slightly in 1972 to 48.1 and rather more in 1973 to 43.9.   The
proportion of all live births to women under 20 increased from 6.2%

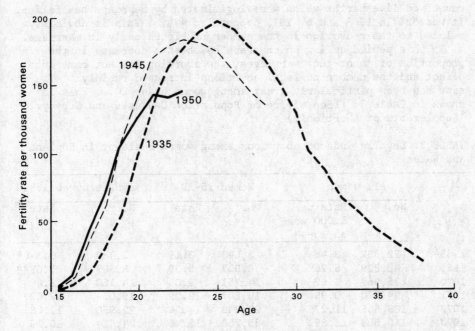

FIGURE 1 Age specific fertility rates for women born in 1935,
1945, 1950 (England and Wales)

in 1959 to 8.8% in 1964, 10.0% in 1968, 10.9% in 1972 and was still
10.8% in 1973.

The changing pattern of births is illustrated in Figure 1 (Farid,
forthcoming) which shows that women born in 1950 have behaved rather
differently from those born in 1945 or 1935.   The 1950 cohort had
a fairly similar pattern of fertility to those born in 1945 until
their twenties.   Then they diverged sharply and have had fewer
children.   Interpretations of this phenomenon differ.   Some see
it merely as a postponement of childbearing, but it could be that a
higher proportion of that cohort both will, and intend to, remain
childless.

This study relates only to married couples with children so to
put it into perspective it is necessary to consider what has been
happening to the marriage rate, the proportion of births occurring
outside marriage, and the proportion of childless couples.

There is some indication that the proportion of childless
couples may be increasing slightly.   Of those married in 1960 18%
were childless after five years of marriage compared with 21% of
those married in 1967 (Farid, 1974).   But among women married when
they were under 20 the proportion who were childless five years
later had changed more markedly: from 10% of those married in 1960
to 15% of those married in 1967.   This may be partly because the
proportion marrying when they were pregnant had fallen.   This fall
has occurred mainly between 1968 and 1972:   38.3% of women married
for the first time when they were under 20 in 1968 had a liveborn
child within eight months, by 1972 this proportion had fallen to

30.8%. For women of all ages the proportion of extra-maritally
conceived live births which were legitimated by marriage has fallen.
It was 52% in 1968 and by 1973 dropped to 47%. This is obviously
related to the reduction in the number of births early in marriage.

  In this period during which there has been a decrease in the
proportion of 'shot-gun' marriages, the abortion law act came into
effect and the number of legal abortions increased rapidly. The
rise has been particularly great among women under 20. This is
shown in Table 3. (See Office of Population Censuses and Surveys,
'Supplements on Abortion'.)

TABLE 3 Legally induced abortions among women resident in England
and Wales

	All women		Women 15-19		Single women 15-19	
	No.	Rate per 1,000 women 15-44	No.	Rate	No.	Rate
1968*	22,332	3.46	3,648	3.19	3,489	3.34**
1969	49,829	5.26	8,907	5.39	8,567	5.69**
1970	75,962	7.97	14,751	9.05	14,160	9.48
1971	94,570	9.98	19,847	12.09	19,054	12.62
1972	108,565	11.27	23,899	14.54	22,950	15.28
1973	110,568	11.39	25,750	15.43	24,614	16.19

* 8 months only.
** Rate per 1,000 single, widowed, divorced and separated women aged
   15-19.

  A summary of abortion and fertility in England and Wales since
1968 (Office of Population Censuses and Surveys, 1974d) describes
the relationship in this way:

  for married women aged 20-29, large falls in numbers of births
  have been associated with comparatively small increases in
  notified abortions; for those aged 40-44, a steady fall in
  births has accompanied a steady rise in notified abortions; and
  for single women aged under 25, births have fallen slightly while
  notified abortions have risen dramatically.

  It seems likely that the fall in the proportion of 'shot-gun'
marriages among teenagers is related to the rise in legal abortions
among young single women. Besides a 'shot-gun' marriage or an
abortion the third possible outcome of a conception outside marriage
is an illegitimate birth. The birth rate among unmarried women
aged 15-44 continued to rise after 1964 and reached its peak, 22.7,
in 1968. It has fallen somewhat and in 1973 was 19.3. As with
legitimate births, the peak in the birth rate among unmarried women
aged 15-19 came rather later than for older women. It was 10.4 in
1964, 14.1 in 1968, highest, 14.6, in 1971, and had fallen slightly,
to 13.6 by 1973. Among this age group the illegitimacy ratio,
that is the proportion of illegitimate births per 100 live births,
has continued its slight rise from 22% in 1964 to 28% in 1973. So
of the three choices open to the pregnant and unmarried women, 'shot-
gun' marriages have become relatively less popular, abortions more
common and the illegitimate birth rate has changed the least.

Overall marriage rates for both bachelors and spinsters reached a peak in 1970 and have declined somewhat since then.   1970 was also the year in which the mean age at marriage was lowest.   The changes are summarized in Table 4.

TABLE 4 Marriage rates and mean age at marriage

	1968	1970	1973
Marriage rate per 1,000 population aged 16 and over			
Bachelors	84.4	86.3	76.6
Spinsters	96.5	100.4	91.8
Mean age at marriage			
Bachelors	24.58	24.43	24.86
Spinsters	22.45	22.38	22.72

The fall in the legitimate birth rate preceded the drop in the marriage rate by six years and the initial fall cannot be attributed to it.   But the decline in marriage rates may have contributed to the steeper fall since 1971.

Another change between 1968 and 1973 is the reduction in the proportion of all births to women who already have three or more children.   This is shown in Table 5.

TABLE 5 Legitimate live births to women married once only by the number of her previous liveborn children

Number of previous liveborn children	1968 %	1970 %	1973 %
0	38.2	39.1	41.9
1	32.5	33.3	36.2
2	15.9	15.7	13.5
3	7.0	6.5	5.0
4	3.2	2.8	1.8
5 or more	3.2	2.6	1.6
Number of births (= 100%)	731,966	700,937	595,443

This reduction in large families has been accompanied by a decrease in the proportion of births to older women of 30 or more. In 1968 the proportion of legitimate births to women of that age was 25%, by 1973 it was 20%.   These two together reflect an earlier termination of child bearing.   At the same time there has been a reduction in fertility rates in the earlier years of marriage (Office of Population Censuses and Surveys, 1972c, p.10).   The proportion of first births to women under 25 fell from 68.0% in 1968 to 67.4% in 1970, then to 59.3% in 1973 (legitimate live births to women married once only).

To sum up, the main demographic trends between the 1967/68 and 1973 studies were:

1 A dramatic fall in the birth rate.
2 An even more dramatic rise in the legal abortion rate.
3 A fall in the proportion of extra-maritally conceived live births
   which were legitimated by marriage.
4 An increase in the proportion of married couples who were
   childless after five years of marriage.
5 A slight decrease in the illegitimate birth rate.
6 A fall in the proportion of births to women who already had
   three or more children.
7 An increase in the proportion of all live births to young women
   under 20 but a decrease in the proportion of first births to
   women under 25.

The increase in childlessness among married women makes the 1973
study somewhat less comprehensive than the 1967/68 one; the
decrease in the illegitimate birth rate makes the later study rather
more comprehensive.

One of the basic problems facing those making predictions about
future trends is the extent to which the fall in the birth rate
represents a postponement of births and the extent to which it
indicates a decrease in family size.   It is hoped that this study
will help them in some small way, but as Hawthorn has put it: 'the
investigation of human fertility, in general, is probably one of the
most extensive sociological industries; judged by its conclusions,
it is perhaps one of the least successful' (Hawthorn, 1974).

Chapter 2

CHANGES BETWEEN 1967/68 AND 1973 AND THE FALL IN THE BIRTH RATE

Although the initial fall in the birth rate after its peak in 1964 resulted from an almost inevitable slow down in the trend to earlier marriage and younger motherhood, the more dramatic and recent fall needs other explanations. There are three main possibilities. One is that there has been a decrease in the number of children people want; another that with more effective contraception and abortion more readily available there has been a decline in the number of unwanted pregnancies and births. A third possibility is that the change has resulted from different spacing patterns - particularly postponement of births until later in marriage. These possibilities are not mutually exclusive and each may be contributing to the fall to some extent. In this chapter the three possibilities are looked at in turn. Data about intentions, contraception, unwanted pregnancy, and spacing patterns in the two surveys, 1967/68 and 1973, are compared in an attempt to assess the extent to which the different factors have contributed to the change.

INTENTIONS

A question about whether they hoped they would have any more children was taken as a basic indicator of their intentions. Feelings about this are strongly related to the number of children they have already, and the proportion of babies born to mothers who already had three or more children fell from 14% in the 1967/68 study to 9% in the 1973 one. (For a discussion of statistical significance see Appendix III.)

Their hopes for further children are compared for families of different sizes in Table 6.

The proportion of mothers who said they hoped they would have more children had fallen by about a third among those with two children and by almost half of those with three. However, among those with two children the proportion who felt uncertain had risen from 10% to 15%. Among those with three children it seems rather more definite that the proportion who wanted more had declined. There is no clear evidence of a change in the proportion who were content with a single-child family. And among the declining

numbers of those with relatively large families of four or more the
proportion who wanted more children had not declined significantly.

But there seems little doubt that between 1967/68 and 1973 there
had been a fall in the number of children married women hoped to
have.   There also seemed to have been a change in their chances of
achieving their wishes.

TABLE 6   Hopes for more children

			Present number of children					
	One		Two		Three		Four or more	
	1967/8	1973	1967/8	1973	1967/8	1973	1967/8	1973
	%	%	%	%	%	%	%	%
Yes	85	82	32	20	20	11	7	5
Uncertain, qualified	6	7	10	15	8	8	8	5
No or cannot	9	11	58	65	72	81	85	90
No.of mothers (= 100%)*	565	600	481	494	219	219	219	129

* The mothers whose baby had died and who did not have any more
  children have been excluded.   There were six on each study.   In
  addition those who were pregnant have been excluded.   There were
  four on the earlier study, sixteen on the present one, including
  one whose only baby had died.   The ten who were widowed, separated
  or divorced on the present study have also been excluded.   One
  mother in the 1967/68 study gave an inadequate response to the
  question about whether she wanted more children and has been
  excluded.

USE OF CONTRACEPTION

In 1967/68 the most common method of contraception for married
parents to have used was the sheath, then withdrawal.   The pill
was in third place followed by the safe period and then the cap.
By 1973 the proportions of parents who said they had ever used the
pill had risen markedly.   Among mothers there was no change in the
proportion ever using the other main methods - the sheath and
withdrawal.   Use of the cap had declined but this had been offset
by an increase in those who had ever used an IUD.   Use of the safe
period had dropped and sterilization risen.   The figures are in
Table 7.

TABLE 7   Methods of contraception - ever used

	Mothers			Fathers		
	1967/68*	1970*	1973	1967/68*	1970	1973
	%	%	%	%		%
Pill	28	40	65	28		62
Cap	17	17	10	16		11
IUD	3	4	8	4		8
Sheath	67	68	69	68		73
Chemicals on own	6	8	8	7		10
Withdrawal	46	45	45	39		47
Safe period	21	15	13	19		16
Male sterilization	}2	}5	3 }7	}2		3 }4
Female sterilization			4			1
Other	7	4	5	7		4
None	7	6	3	8		4
Number of mothers or fathers (= 100%)**	1,482	232	1,464	257		262

* From 'Parents and Family Planning Services'.
** Small numbers for whom inadequate information was obtained have been omitted in this and in subsequent tables.

The picture from the fathers is similar except that they less often reported female sterilization.   The discrepancy in the reported use of withdrawal by mothers and fathers in the earlier study is not repeated in the present study.   It seems unlikely that the proportion using withdrawal had risen; it was probably under-reported by fathers before.   One difference in methods is that fathers were interviewed by men on the earlier study and by women in the present one.

Changes in their current use of contraception, shown in Table 8, are even more marked.

By 1973 the pill was easily the most popular method of contraception for married couples a few months after they had a baby. The fact that there was no change in the proportion currently using the pill between 1967/68 and 1970 was probably the result of the 'scare' at the end of 1969 (Scowen, 1969).   Mothers currently taking the pill as a proportion of those who had ever taken it was 71% in 1967/68, 50% in 1970 and 66% in 1973.

Current use of withdrawal, as reported by mothers, has fallen dramatically;   use of the sheath rather less so but quite appreciably.   Use of sterlization had increased even more proportionately than that of the pill.   Of the mothers, 4.4% said in 1973 that they had been sterilized, 3.3% that their husbands had been.   The ratio reported by the fathers was in the opposite direction but this difference might have arisen by chance.

Data from the recalls indicate that, apart from sterilization, there may be fairly frequent changes in the method of contraception used during the five-twelve months after the birth of the baby. Sixteen %   of the mothers who reported that they were taking the pill at the first interview were no longer doing so when seen two to five months later.   But those who had given it up had been 'replaced' by others who were previously using different methods. The proportion using the sheath on the other hand had declined during that time - from 23% to 18%.

To sum up, in 1973 a much higher proportion of married couples were using relatively reliable methods of contraception than in 1967/68.   At the later time four-fifths were using the pill, coil, cap, sheath or sterilization compared with two-thirds five years earlier.

TABLE 8   Present use of contraception

	Mothers			Fathers		
	1967/68*	1970*	1973	1967/68*	1970	1973
	%	%	%	%		%
Pill	20	20	43	21		44
Cap	5	4	2	2		2
IUD	3	3	6	4		5
Sheath	36	33	23	39		25
Chemicals on own	1	3	1	2		2
Withdrawal	21	22	8	12		11
Safe period	6	7	3	5		2
Male sterilization	}2	}5	3 }7	}2		3 }4
Female sterilization			4			1
Other	2	1	1	2		-
None	16	13	11	20		11
Number of mothers or fathers (= 100%)**	1,477	233	1,457	257		263

*   From 'Parents and Family Planning Services'.
** Percentages add to more than 100 as some parents reported that they were currently using more than one method.

UNINTENDED PREGNANCIES

If people were using more reliable contraceptives did this lead to a reduction in unintended pregnancies?   The proportion of mothers who said they were using some method of birth control round about the time they became pregnant with the survey baby was 22% on the 1973 survey, compared with 29% on the earlier one - a significant reduction.   At the same time there was little change in their reported reactions when they first found they were pregnant.   The question on both studies asked: 'Apart from what you feel now - looking back to the time when you first found you were pregnant - at the time would you rather it had happened a bit earlier or later or were you pleased you were pregnant then or sorry it happened at all?'   Replies are shown in Table 9.

TABLE 9 Attitudes to pregnancy

	1967/68	1973
	%	%
Pleased	61	63
Rather earlier	7	10
Rather later	17	14
Sorry it happened at all	15	13
Number of mothers (= 100%)	1,473	1,461

There was no difference in the proportion who said they felt
pleased or sorry at the start of their pregnancy.   This is in
spite of the increase in legal abortions, in spite of the decrease
in large families of four or more, and in spite of the increased
use of more reliable methods of contraception.
    Reactions to pregnancy are strongly related to the number of
children a mother has already, and it has already been shown that
the proportion with large families decreased between the two studies.
Table 10 suggests that the smaller proportion of mothers having four
or more children has been accompanied by an increase in the
proportion of those having a fourth baby who regretted the pregnancy
initially, a further indication of a lower level of intentions in
recent years.   There were no significant changes in the proportions
who were 'pleased' or 'sorry' in the other family size groups.

TABLE 10 Family size and attitudes to previous pregnancy

	Size of family									
	One		Two		Three		Four		Five or more	
	1967/8	1973	1967/8	1973	1967/8	1973	1967/8	1973	1967/8	1973
	%	%	%	%	%	%	%	%	%	%
Pleased pregnant then	66	67	72	70	45	50	44	32	41	39
Rather earlier	7	10	9	12	6	9	5	8	1	2
Rather later	23	19	14	13	15	6	11	5	6	7
Sorry it happened at all	4	4	5	5	34	35	40	55	52	52
Number of mothers (= 100%)	562	606	478	502	216	220	105	75	108	54

SPACING

In the more recent study there was an overall decrease in the
proportion of births which the mothers said they would have liked
to have had later and an increase in those they would have preferred
to be earlier.   Table 10 showed that for all family sizes except
those of five or more the proportion of mothers who said they would
have preferred the last baby to be born earlier had increased
between 1967/68 and 1973, and the proportion preferring it later had
decreased, although not all the differences reached the level of
statistical significance.   This might suggest that there had been
an increasing preference for short birth intervals or for starting
families earlier.   But there was no indication that mothers wanted
a shorter interval before their next baby in 1973 than in 1967/68.
Nor was there any indication that births were occurring closer
together. (Unfortunately the data from the two studies about this
are not entirely comparable.   In the 1967/68 survey a pregnancy
history was obtained with the dates of all pregnancies and
miscarriages.   The interval was calculated in months between the
end of the two pregnancies - if the last one was a live birth - or
between the month when the previous pregnancy would have ended if
it was a miscarriage.   In the 1973 survey information relates to
the interval between the survey baby and the previous liveborn child.)
    A possible explanation is that in 1973 with the increasing use
of effective contraception fewer mothers were becoming pregnant
earlier than they intended.   This would account for the fall in
the proportion saying they wished the pregnancy had been later.
If at the same time there has been a trend towards an increasing
preference for shorter intervals between births the actual
distribution of space intervals might remain unchanged - the
decrease in unwanted short intervals being made up by an increase
in wanted ones.   Two observations remain unexplained: the increase
in the proportion who would have preferred their previous pregnancy
to have occurred earlier and the lack of difference in the preferred
interval before the next baby.   Mothers who said they would have
preferred their pregnancies to be earlier might mean they had
experienced delays in becoming pregnant, or that their preferences
for an earlier pregnancy had been deliberately outweighed by other
considerations, or that they had not intended to become pregnant
but since it had happened they wished it had been earlier.   The
time it took them to become pregnant in 1973, shown in Table 11,
suggests that the deferment was unplanned for about half of them
as it took them a year or longer. ('For how long had you been
having intercourse without taking any precautions - up until you
became pregnant?')
    For the others it may be that more of them in 1973 than in
1967/68 had deliberately postponed their pregnancy, for economic or
other reasons, but had subsequently regretted the postponement. If
they feel more able to control their fertility and particularly
their final family size people may be more inclined for that reason
to want their children close together but economic pressures may
act in the opposite direction.

TABLE 11   Attitudes to pregnancy and time taken to become pregnant

	Attitude to spacing		
	Pleased pregnant then	Rather earlier	Rather later
Length of time having unprotected intercourse	%	%	%
Less than 3 months	54	18	47
3 months < 1 year	31	31	35
1 year < 2 years	7	15	10
2 years or longer	8	36	8
Number of mothers not using any method of birth control when became pregnant (=100%)	810	132	116

Another aspect of spacing is the age at which people have their children. In 1973 fewer mothers were starting their families before they were 25 than in 1968.   This was clear from the national statistics discussed in the previous chapter, and is likely to influence their final family size.   In general hopes for further children tended to decrease with increasing age.   This is shown in Table 12 for those with two children.   The variation with length of marriage is also shown.

TABLE 12   Hopes for a third child by age and length of marriage

	Proportion of those with two children who hoped they would have another	
	1967/68	1973
Age of mother		
Under 20	*	42% (24)
20-24	44% (133)	29% (194)
25-29	38% (225)	17% (195)
30 or more	23% (107)	11% (85)
Length of marriage		
Less than 2 years	45% (22)	38% (56)
2 years < 3 years	57% (49)	30% (88)
3 years < 4 years	35% (79)	21% (85)
4 years < 5 years	34% (93)	20% (91)
5 years < 10 years	36% (191)	15% (156)
10 years or longer	11% (46)	8% (24)

Numbers in brackets are those on which percentages are based (= 100%)
* Numbers too small

There is a clear trend with age on both studies and within age groups the fall between the two studies is more marked.   With length of marriage the trend was clear and smooth in 1973 but less well marked in the earlier study.

These figures suggest that mothers wanting three or more children tend to concentrate their childbearing in the early years of marriage and that an increase in childlessness in the early years of marriage is likely to be associated with a desire for a two-child family among those who do have children.

THE CONUNDRUM

The puzzle from these findings is that although parents were using more effective methods of contraception in 1973 than in 1967/68, and legal abortions were so much more available, there was apparently no change in the proportion of legitimate births resulting from pregnancies which were initially unwelcome.

One possibility is that the question about their initial feelings about their pregnancy may be eliciting a set response rather than reflecting changes in attitudes and perceptions.   Some people may be inclined to respond to an event with pleasure and others with regret and these responses may not be affected by their situation so that the proportions expressing these viewpoints could remain stable even though intentions and the use of birth control around the time of conception differed.   This interpretation does not seem tenable since the proportion of mothers who said they felt sorry their pregnancy happened at all varied markedly with their family size in both 1967/68 and 1973, from less than one in twenty of those with no previous children to over half of those with five or more children already, although it may be argued that mothers may feel it is more acceptable to express regret about a pregnancy when they already have several children than if they do not have any.

A more plausible explanation is that people's expectations about their ability to control their pregnancies had changed, so that pregnancies which would earlier have been accepted even though not planned were more recently regarded with concern or dismay.   In the later survey fewer pregnancies were said to have occurred while people were attempting some form of birth control.   This is probably because people were using more efficient methods of contraception.   But as their desire for more children had fallen so had their tolerance of unintended pregnancy.   It is also possible that the increase in the proportion who said they wished their pregnancy had happened earlier reflects a rise in expectations about their ability to control and time their pregnancies.

In relation to the fall in the birth rate, these data suggest that parents are now wanting smaller families and their chances of controlling their fertility have increased.   There is no evidence from these studies to indicate that people are spacing their births more widely.   The nature of the samples precludes any information about an increase in childlessness.

Chapter 3

NATURE OF INTENTIONS

To what extent and at what stage do parents have definite intentions about possible children?   In an attempt to explore these questions this chapter looks at some indicators of their past and future intentions about family size and at their preferences for children of a particular sex or families of a particular sex composition.

One major difficulty is that asking people questions about their intentions may seem to imply that they should have plans, whereas of course some people, at any rate at certain stages of their lives and marriages, may not have any.   Another problem is the wide variety in the possible nature of people's intentions, which again means that if questions are asked about the precise nature of some intentions, parents who do not plan in this way may react by pretending they have done so.   A third difficulty is that people may have feelings and intentions which are apparently inconsistent. When questions seem likely to reveal this they may adjust their answers to present a more logical picture.   Finally, the questioning at the interview may take some people through what is effectively a decision-making process.   An illustration of a number of these problems is given by one interview:

A woman with one daughter initially said she did not want any more children, but then that she might possibly change her mind because 'I might get beaten into submission - might have one in a mad moment.'   Later when the interviewer, incorrectly according to the instructions, asked her how many children she would like to have altogether she said 'two'.

INTENTIONS ABOUT FAMILY SIZE AT TIME OF MARRIAGE

Obviously views about the number of children wanted may alter during the course of a marriage and so, almost inevitably, people's perceptions about their views at the time of marriage are likely to change.   Nevertheless questions about this probably give some indication of the direction, if not the size, of people's changing intentions.   In this study parents were asked: 'Looking back to the time when you got married, at that time, did you yourself think you would like to have any children sometime? Had you any idea how many?'   Replies are given in Table 13 for both mothers and fathers. Results are also compared with those from 'Parents and Family Planning Services', although the question in the earlier study was slightly different. ('When you first got married, did you want any children? How many?')

TABLE 13   Number of children mothers and fathers said they had wanted when they first married

	Mothers		Fathers	
	1967/68	1973	1967/68	1973
	%	%	%	%
None	4	5	3	2
Wanted one	5	3	4	2
One or two	-	2	-	2
Two	39	40	37	51
Two or three	4	6	6	8
Three (inc. three or four)	15 ⎤	10 ⎤	22 ⎤	9 ⎤
Four (inc. four or five)	16 ⎬37	11 ⎬24	9 ⎬35	5 ⎬15
Five or more, several, big family	6 ⎦	3 ⎦	4 ⎦	1 ⎦
Some - uncertain how many	⎫	19	⎫	20
Uncertain if wanted any	⎭11	1	⎭15	-
Number of mothers or fathers (= 100%)	1,477	1,470	252	262

   Between 1967/68 and 1973 there were no significant changes in the proportions of parents who said they had not wanted any children nor in the proportions who wanted one, but the proportions wanting three or more had fallen from 37% to 24% of mothers and even more from 35% to 15% of fathers. More of the fathers in 1973 than in 1967/68 said they wanted two children (Peel and Carr, 1975, p.47). Among the mothers there was an increase in uncertainty at the later study. This ties in with the observation in the previous chapter, that a higher proportion of those with two children were uncertain whether they wanted a third child or not. Although hopes or intentions are for fewer children, in 1973 they seemed to be less firmly held than previously. This seems understandable at a time of rapid change.
   Another way to look at possible trends is to see whether people's reported intentions varied with the year in which they were married (which for this sample is directly related to the length of their marriage). The difficulty with this comparison is the possible confusion between time and generation effects. Those who had been married for longer were being asked to recall their reactions after a greater interval. Time may distort recollections in different ways. Some may say they wanted some children but did not know how many because they have forgotten how many they wanted then; for others subsequent events may impose on their memories, so they become more definite about the numbers they wanted in the

past.   In practice we found that the proportion of mothers who said
they wanted some children but had no idea how many was 21% of those
married for less than two years, fell to 16% of those married
between two and ten years, then rose to 31% of those married for ten
years or longer.   Among those mentioning a number (two or three was
taken as 2.5) the average increased from 2.14 of those married less
than a year to 2.51 of those married for ten or more years.   This
again suggests a fall in family size aspirations among those married
more recently.

Mothers who said they had wanted some children at the time of
their marriage were also asked about the smallest and about the
largest number they had thought they might like.   The average for
the smallest was 2.06, for the largest 3.03, with 35% giving the
same answer in response to both questions.   So, many mothers felt
that at the start of their marriage they did not have clear
intentions about the number of children they wanted.   They had
open minds to the extent of an average of almost one child.

Mothers who said they had not wanted any children at the time of
their marriage had, as a group, a rather longer interval between
marriage and their first birth than other mothers - a quarter of
them waited four or more years compared with a tenth of other
mothers.   When asked why they had changed their minds, two-fifths
said they had not done so:
    'It was unplanned. I didn't change my mind - this baby was a
    mistake.'
    'Well, I was unlucky and got caught.'
    'I didn't really change my mind until I was having her.   Then
    I was thrilled to bits.'
    'We didn't plan. I just conceived - but I had no maternal
    longings.'
A third said they had come to regard it as an integral part of
being married - wanting a family and settling down:
    'I think once you are married you feel differently.'
    'I found with both of us working there was no family life without
    children.'
Some, who have been included in this last group, saw children as a
way of helping their marriage:
    'Our life was getting a bit humdrum - both working, getting a
    bit fed up with each other.'
A sixth had been influenced by their husbands:
    'I didn't change my mind but my husband thinks you can't be
    happy if you haven't got children so I agreed.'
And a tenth by their friends:
    'My friend was having a baby. She was a very close friend, and
    with all the excitement I said to my husband, let us have one
    too.'
About one in ten gave more than one reason.

Of course, this sample does not cover all those who did not want
any children when they first married - only those who either changed
their minds or who became pregnant by mistake and then did not get
an abortion.   The basic denominator cannot be estimated from this
study but other inquiries (Langford, forthcoming; Peel and Carr,
1975, p.41) suggest that possibly around 4% of couples getting
married may intend not to have any children.   In this case data

from the present survey suggest that the majority of them change
their minds or have an unplanned birth.   But of course others who
initially intend to have children may change their minds and decide
not to do so, and others will not have children although they would
like to do so.

Bearing in mind the limitations of the data about parents'
retrospective reports of their feelings at the time of marriage,
they suggest:

1 The numbers of children couples want at the time of marriage
   have been declining.
2 At the time of marriage many couples are uncertain about the
   number of children they want.
3 A substantial proportion who do not want children at the time
   of their marriage will have some.

PRESENT INTENTIONS ABOUT FAMILY SIZE

Other studies of people's intentions about family size have
questioned people about the number of children they want, the
number they expect to have, and their perceptions of ideal family
size. (Myra Woolf in 'Family Intentions' asked married women about
the number of children they considered ideal for families with no
particular worries about money, and about the number they expected.
Whelpton, Campbell and Patterson in 'Fertility and Family Planning
in the United States' asked about the ideal number of children for
the average American family, the desired number and the number
expected.)   The concept of ideal family size may be helpful in
understanding the factors that influence people to want or expect
different numbers from their perceived ideal.   Expectations are
used as a measure of ultimate family size.   They attempt to take
into account fecundity impairments, unwillingness or inability to
prevent unwanted pregnancies and differences in family size
preferences between husbands and wives.   There is still the problem
that expectations are likely to vary at different stages of a
marriage.   In this study, for an initial indication of people's
intentions, they were asked simply whether they hoped they would
have any more children.   But even with this limited and relatively
straightforward question there were problems.   Some people
apparently answered in terms of the immediate future.   When asked
whether they thought they might even change their mind about this,
only two, less than 1%, of those who said they hoped they would
have more children thought they might ever change their mind about
this, but a third of those who said they did not want any more
thought they might change their mind at some stage.   This
proportion was nearly two-thirds among those with only one child
who said they did not want any more, and fell to one in seven among
those with four or more - a further indication of people's
uncertainty about a one-child family.   When they were asked what
sort of thing might make them change their mind, 43% of those who
said they might do so just said they might change their minds later
on, when they or their children were older:

  'Well, I'm saying this now, but you never know in ten years'
  time. We've got a boy and a girl which is what everyone wants.

It is a reasonable sized family. At the moment I don't think
I would change my mind, not really.'
Nineteen per cent said they might do so if they had more money or
if they, or their husband, had a better job.
'It's a matter of affording them. It's difficult enough with
him really, and I want him to have everything. If we could
afford it - at the present it's out of the question.'
Fourteen per cent might do so if they could be sure of getting a
baby of a particular sex:
'I don't think so at the moment. I would love a boy but I
wouldn't want three girls. I don't really want any more - but
I might change my mind.'
Thirteen per cent said they would do so if anything happened to
their present children, 10% said they might change their mind
because they liked children:
'We've got one of each and we can't afford more - but probably
when these two get older - I've got used to having children
about and I might miss them.'
Seven per cent might change if they had more suitable housing:
'Not for a long time. I've no room, have to wait for a council
place. I don't really want any more. I had to have a Caesarian
and the doctor said I'd have to wait a bit. I like kids but I
don't like having them.'
Some other comments were:
'My husband wants another one but I want to go out to work then.'
'Financial - I've got a career as well. If we had a lot more
money or if my job packed up I suppose.'
And as the comments have illustrated, several mothers mentioned more
than one possibility.
   In addition to the 15% of all mothers who thought they might
change their mind about not having any more children, 10% said they
were uncertain about whether or not they wanted more.   Those who
were uncertain and those who said they wanted more were asked how
many they wanted altogether.('Could you say about how many children
you would like to have altogether?') Replies are shown in Table 14.

TABLE 14 Final family size

	Average number of children	
	Hoped for	Already obtained
Those who hoped for more	2.61 (640)	1.27 (646)
Those who were uncertain if they wanted more	2.72 (129)	1.97 (140)
Those who did not want more and might change mind		2.19 (221)
Those who did not want more and would not change mind		2.80 (456)

Figures in brackets are the numbers of mothers on which the averages
are based.

Those who did not want any more children and said they would not
change their mind about this already had slightly more children on
average than were wanted by those who reckoned they had not yet
completed their families or were uncertain about this.   However,
those who said they did not want more but might change their minds
only had an average of 2.19 children, fewer than the number wanted
by those who hoped for more or were uncertain.

Of the mothers who initially said they were uncertain whether
they wanted more, two-thirds said at a later question that the
number they would like to have altogether was greater than the
number they had at the moment, a fifth said it was the same as they
already had, and one in eight were still uncertain.   This suggests
that the majority, possibly three-quarters, may decide to have
another one later.   On the other hand, data from the recalls
showed that two to five months after the interview a third of the
mothers who had said they were uncertain about wanting another baby
were still uncertain, a third said they hoped they would have
another, and a third that they did not want another.   Repeating
the same question at a later date, and with a different interviewer
who had no knowledge of what was said at the first interview,
probably gives a better indication of the strength of people's
intentions than a second, slightly different, question at the same
interview.   Mothers may have felt they had already expressed their
doubts about wanting another baby when they told us they were
uncertain whether they hoped they would have another or not.   So
when asked to say 'about how many children' they would like to have
altogether they may have tended to give a maximum answer.

Some idea of the range of people's uncertainties is given in
Table 15, which shows the smallest and the largest number of children
mothers said they would like to have.   Those who did not want any
more have been included at the number they already have for both
dimensions.   Those who were uncertain whether or not they wanted
more have been included at the number they already have for the
smallest number.   The difference in averages ranged from 2.47 for
the smallest to 2.75 for the largest, assuming half of those who
were uncertain had an additional child, and 2.80 assuming all those
who were uncertain had an additional child.   So uncertainty about
the number of children wanted amounted, on average, to about a third
of a child.

TABLE 15   Range of number of children wanted

Smallest	Largest						Uncertain	All mothers
	1	2	3	4	5	6 or more		
1	4%	2%					2%	8%
2		38%	10%	3%	1%		4%	56%
3			18%	2%			3%	23%
4				9%				9%
5					2%			2%
6 or more						2%		2%
All mothers	4%	40%	28%	14%	3%	2%	9%	1,462 = 100%

Among the mothers who hoped for more children, their final desired family size was 2.90 children in the 1967/68 survey compared with 2.61 in the present survey, while the numbers they already had, among those who did not want any more, had fallen from 2.99 on average in 1967/68 to 2.60 in 1973. (The averages for desired and completed family size are high because of the bias in the sample - it will be recalled that the average completed family size in the 1973 sample would be of the order of 2.93 compared with 2.40 in the population from which it was drawn because of this bias.) So this is further evidence of a fall in the number of children wanted but there is clearly quite a lot of uncertainty not only about the final number wanted but also about whether they wanted another child.

CHANGES IN INTENTIONS

Among mothers hoping for more children at the time of interview, the majority, 83% wanted about the same number of children as they did at the time of their marriage, 9% now wanted more children than when they got married, and 8% fewer. (Those giving a range for the number wanted at the time of marriage have been taken as wanting the same family size if the number fell within that range.) So overall there was no significant change in the numbers wanted in this group taken together. But among those who did not want any more 61% now had the same number as they wanted at the time of marriage, 26% had more and 13% fewer than they had wanted at the time of their marriage. So for them the trend has been to a larger family size. In 1967/68 the comparable proportions among those who did not want any more children were 46% with the same number as they wanted when they first married, 35% with more and 19% with fewer - an indication of a reduction in unintended pregnancies.

Reasons for having, or wanting, fewer children than they did at the time of marriage were first cost, mentioned by 44% of the mothers in this group, then problems of bringing up children mentioned by 35%, and fear or dislike of pregnancy or childbirth, by 31%. Housing was given as a reason by 6% and there were a variety of other reasons. Some gave more than one.

The most common explanation for having more children than they had wanted at the time of marriage was that it just happened - it was a mistake. Half the mothers in this category said this.

'After Jenny we did try to prevent them and I went on the pill but it didn't agree with me. While I was waiting to be fitted with the coil after I'd come off the pill I fell for Angela. Then after Angela I was fitted with the coil and had to have it removed - then I fell for David.'

Other reasons for having or wanting more children were enjoyment of children given by 24%, and pressures from husband mentioned by 9% of the mothers. Again a number gave more than one reason:

'I like babies. I'm a bit of an optimist - always thought I wouldn't become pregnant. I take what comes and accept it.'

Twelve per cent wanted a child of a particular sex - or a combination of sexes in their family, and had or wanted additional children in an attempt to achieve this.

SEX PREFERENCES

Parents' desires for a child of a particular sex or for a combination, a particular distribution of sexes in their family, are of
interest to demographers at the moment because, as has just been
shown, these preferences may influence the number of children
people decide to have.   In the future, if it becomes possible for
people to choose the sex of their children, their preferences will
affect the sex distribution of children and the numbers of children.
The influence on the numbers is likely to be rather different from
the effect of preferences at the moment.   Initially it might lead
to an increase in births, as more parents who would like a
particular sex would probably decide to have one if they could be
sure of getting what they want.   In the long run it would probably
lead to a decrease as parents would not need to have additional
children to try and get the sex or sex distribution they wanted.
      Parents who said that when they married they thought they would
like to have children sometime were asked if they had any sex
preferences at that time.   ('What about boys and girls, did you
have any views on that?')   A third of the mothers said no, a
quarter said they had wanted one of each, and another sixth some
of each, a tenth said they had wanted a boy or boys, and one in
thirteen a girl or girls.   Fourteen per cent were concerned about
which they had first, the majority of these, 10%, wanting a boy
first.
      Again there is the possibility that subsequent events may have
influenced people's perceptions of their views at an earlier point
in time.   But the evidence suggests that this had not happened to
any marked extent.   Comparing those with single-sex families,
there was no difference between those with girls and those with
boys in the proportions who said they had wanted boy(s) or girl(s)
at the time of their marriage - but more of those with a boy or
boys said they had wanted a boy first: 12% compared with 6% of
those with a girl or girls.   When single-sex and mixed-sex
families were compared, the proportion saying that at the time of
their marriage they wanted a family with both boy(s) and girl(s)
was 18% among those who had such a family, 13% among the others.
In theory, this difference may have occurred because they were
prepared to have more children in order to achieve their aims, but
in practice there was no difference in the current family size of
those who said they had wanted a mixed sex family and those who had
felt a preference for a particular sex.
      Those who said at the interview that they hoped they would have
more children, or were uncertain about this, were asked if they
had any preference about the sex.   ('Would you prefer the next one
to be a boy or a girl, or don't you mind?')   Both the mothers and
fathers fell into three equal-sized groups: those preferring a
boy, those preferring a girl, and those who did not mind.   Among
both mothers and fathers there was no indication of a preference
in favour of one sex rather than another.   This is shown in
Table 16.

TABLE 16   Sex preferences for next baby and sex composition of present family

	Mothers' Present family			Fathers' Present family		
	Boy(s) only	Girl(s) only	Boy(s) and girl(s)	Boy(s) only	Girl(s) only	Boy(s) and girl(s)
Prefer next baby to be:	%	%	%	%	%	%
Boy	7	63	31	4	73	
Girl	62	7	21	71	4	*
Don't mind	31	30	48	25	23	
No. of parents wanting another baby (= 100%)	338	334	98	72	55	(14)

* Numbers too small.

Parents were less likely to have a preference if they already had a child of each sex.   Demographically the important question is whether desire for a child of a particular sex influences the number of children a couple has.   We asked those expressing a preference whether, if they did not get the sex they wanted next time, this might affect the number they decided to have.   Just over a quarter, 27%, of those expressing a preference said that it might, 6% were uncertain, two-thirds said it would not.   As a proportion of all those who hoped or might hope for another child, just under a fifth, 18%, said the sex of the next baby might influence the number they decided to have.   This proportion was 20% of single-sex families (with no difference between those with all boys and those will all girls) and 6% of mixed-sex ones.

Table 17 shows the relationship between the number of additional children wanted and the mothers' views on whether the sex of the next baby might affect the number they decided to have.   Not surprisingly, those who were uncertain whether they wanted one or two more were most likely to be influenced by the sex of the next baby.   Those who had said they only wanted one more were least likely to say the sex of the baby might influence them about this - but almost a fifth thought it might do so.   A third of those who said they wanted two or more additional children thought the final number would depend on the sex they got.

TABLE 17   Number of additional children desired by whether the sex of next one was thought likely to affect the number they have

Sex of next baby likely to affect final number	Number of additional children wanted		
	One	One or two	Two or more
	%	%	%
Yes	18	76	34
No	76	17	64
Uncertain	6	7	2
Number of mothers (= 100%)	343	54	101

But of course it is difficult for people to predict how they will feel and act after a future event.   Another way to look at the possible effect of the desire that many couples have for children of both sexes is to look at the hopes for more children in families of different sex compositions.   This is done in Table 18.

TABLE 18   Variations in hopes for more children with present sex composition of family

	Two children in family		Three or more children in family	
	Single sex	Mixed sexes	Single sex	Mixed sexes
Hopes for more	%	%	%	%
Yes	26	17	16	7
Uncertain	19	9	9	7
No – but might change mind	21	28	15	17
No – will not change mind	34	46	60	69
Number of mothers (= 100%)	268	234	74	274

In single-sex families there was no difference between those with boys only and those with girls only in the proportion wanting more children, but in families with two or more children, a higher proportion of those with single-sex families than of those with mixed-sex ones hoped to have another child.   Similar differences existed for fathers whose preference was also for children of both sexes and whose desire for further children did not vary between those with boys only and those with girls only.

Comparisons with unpublished data from the survey for 'Parents and Family Planning Services' suggest that, among parents with three children, in the more recent 1973 survey their desires for smaller families took a greater precedence over their preference for

a mixed-sex family than it did among the families surveyed five
years earlier.   However, among families with two children the
relative difference between those with single- and mixed-sex
families in the proportion who hoped to have a further child was
fairly similar in the two studies.   These conclusions are drawn
from the information in Table 19.

TABLE 19   Changes over time in the influence of sex preferences

	Two-child families				Three-child families			
	1967/68		1973		1967/68		1973	
	Single sex	Mixed sex	Single sex	Mixed sex	Single sex	Mixed sex	Single sex	Mixed sex
Hopes for more %	%	%	%	%	%	%	%	%
Yes	35	27	26	17	38	14	16	9
Uncertain	13	7	19	9	13	9	10	8
No	52	66	55	74	49	77	74	83
No. of mothers (= 100%)	255	225	268	234	60	160	63	156
Ratio of the proportion wanting more among single-sex families divided by proportion wanting more in mixed-sex families	1.3		1.5		2.7		1.8	

This suggests that there has been no change in the influence of sex
preferences on the decision to have three rather than two children,
but the influence on the decision in larger families has declined.
But, from a demographic viewpoint, the decision to have three
rather than two is of primary importance in England today.   The
data about their hopes for another child and predictions about
future intentions suggest that a desire for a mixed-sex family
contributes to that decision.   But what of their actions?   If
parents with two children of the same sex are more likely to have
a third child than those with a boy and a girl then the sex mix of
the first two children in families with three or more children would
be expected to show an excess of single-sex pairs over mixed-sex
pairs.   In practice there were 96 families of three or more children
with two boys in the first two, 95 with two girls and 159 with one
of each - a difference in the expected direction but one which might
have occurred by chance.

INTENTIONS ABOUT SURVEY BABIES

It has already been shown that the main reason for mothers having more children than they wanted at the time of their marriage was that they became pregnant when they did not want to be.   Data from a number of studies show that many pregnancies are not planned and are initially unwelcome.   Estimates vary with the definition, but Bone (1973) reported that half, 52%, of the pregnancies occurring to the married couples in her sample were planned in the sense that the couples stopped contraception in order to conceive, and in 'Parents and Family Planning Services' a similar proportion, 53%, of legitimate births resulted from pregnancies which the mothers reported they had been pleased about initially and for which they were not using any form of birth control.   The proportion on the present study was also similar, 57%.

Many, possibly most, women have mixed feelings when they find they are pregnant, and their reactions to their pregnancy are likely to change at different stages.   Some indication of this is given in Table 20, which shows that 6% of the mothers said they were pleased when they found they were pregnant although they had been attempting some form of birth control around the time of conception.   One in eight of the mothers had not been attempting to control their fertility but did not apparently wish to become pregnant either at all or at that point in time.   Actions over preventing pregnancy therefore seemed inconsistent with their initial reactions to the pregnancy for about a fifth of the mothers.

TABLE 20   Reactions to pregnancy and use of contraception around time of conception

	%
Pleased, not using any method of birth control	57
Preferred earlier, not using any method of birth control	9
Pleased, using some method of birth control	6
Preferred earlier, using some method of birth control	1
Preferred later, not using any method of birth control	8
Sorry it happened at all, not using any method of birth control	5
Preferred later, using a method of birth control	6
Sorry it happened at all, using a method of birth control	8
Number of mothers (= 100%)	1,458

An additional question on the present study asked mothers whether they would say they intended to become pregnant that time or not. Sixty-five per cent said they did.   This proportion was 80% among those not attempting any method of birth control around the time they conceived, 9% among the others.   Looking at this the other way round, 3% of those who said they intended to become pregnant were using some method of birth control, 56% of those who said they did not intend to were doing so.   Clearly many married couples have unprotected intercourse when they do not intend to become pregnant.

Altogether 61% of the mothers said about the conception leading

to the survey baby that they were not using any method of contraception, they intended to get pregnant, and they were either
pleased they were pregnant then or would have preferred to be
pregnant earlier.   At the other end of the scale 14% were using
some method of birth control, did not intend to become pregnant,
and were either 'sorry it happened at all' when they found they
were pregnant or would have liked the pregnancy to be later.   This
leaves a quarter of the mothers with reactions which were mixed or
'inconsistent' with their actions.

To sum up, mothers' intentions about their pregnancy which led
to the survey baby were looked at in five different ways: 35% were
said to be unintended, 22% were accidental in that they occurred
when some method of contraception was being attempted, 13% were
regretted in that the mothers felt 'sorry they happened at all',
24% were wrongly spaced (10% being later, 14% earlier than the
mothers would have wished), and taking all these together, 52% were
intended, not accidental, and the mothers were pleased the pregnancy
happened when it did.

The proportion of mothers who said they felt 'sorry it happened
at all' rose from one in twenty of those having their first or
second child to a third of those having their third and just over
half having their fourth or later child.   This is seen in Table 21.

TABLE 21 Number of children and intentions about survey baby

	Number of mother's own children - including survey baby				
	One	Two	Three	Four	Five or more
Initial reactions to pregnancy:	%	%	%	%	%
Pleased pregnant then	67	70	50	32	39
Rather earlier	10	12	9	8	2
Rather later	19	13	6	5	7
Sorry it happened at all	4	5	35	55	52
Using method of birth control around time of conception:	%	%	%	%	%
Yes	14	17	41	47	41
No	86	83	59	53	59
Intended to become pregnant that time:	%	%	%	%	%
Yes	71	77	41	30	29
No	29	23	59	70	71
No.of mothers(=100%)*	610	503	222	77	55

* Small numbers for whom inadequate information was obtained have
  been excluded when calculating percentages.

The main difference in the proportion using a method of birth control around the time they became pregnant was between those having their second and their third babies.   Differences in this proportion among mothers having their third, fourth or later babies might have occurred by chance.   But a smaller proportion of fourth, or later, than of third pregnancies were welcome or intended.   The proportion of pregnancies that were regretted (the mother said she felt 'sorry it happened at all') but which occurred when no method of birth control was being used was 2% of first and second births, 10% of third ones and 21% of later ones.

SUMMARY

This chapter has illustrated some of the complexities of parents' family intentions and the difficulties in assessing them.   It has also looked at the way intentions vary both over time and at different stages of a marriage, and at the extent to which intentions are achieved.   The main findings are that a substantial proportion of couples do not have any definite intentions at the time of their marriage about the number of children they want, and even after the birth of the survey babies a quarter of the mothers expressed some uncertainty about whether or not they wanted another child.   The number of children wanted in 1973 had declined from the earlier study in 1967/68, and among mothers with three or more children desire for a mixed-sex family was by then less likely to lead to an additional child;   however, for those with two children this still appeared to be an important influence.   In this sample parents were likely to have rather more children than they intended, and nearly half, 48% of the pregnancies leading to the survey babies were either unintended, accidental, initially regretted, or wrongly spaced.

Chapter 4

TIMING AND SPACING

The age at which people have their first baby and the space between births have short- and long-term implications for birth rates and population sizes. Three aspects of timing are considered here - the stage at which people get married, the interval between marriage and first pregnancy and the interval between births.

TIME OF MARRIAGE

To try and get some idea why people marry when they do mothers were asked why they decided to get married when they did and not, say, a year earlier or later. The three most common types of reason, each given by a fifth of the mothers, were money, housing, and pregnancy.
   Most of those who quoted financial reasons for getting married when they did had waited to save up for it.
      'We saved up and when we'd enough we got married - we didn't
      want to wait any longer.'
A few had married earlier than they would otherwise have done because of an unexpected windfall.
      'I got made redundant and from the money we got we decided to
      marry.   It came a bit soon but we were planning to marry anyway.'
Housing reasons seemed more evenly balanced in terms of postponing or bringing forward marriage dates.
      'A year earlier I was only 15. I wasn't happy at home so moved
      in with his parents. We were going to get married later but
      as we were living in the same house there was no point in waiting.'
      'The house was available at that June - we had nowhere to live
      before.'
      'Earlier the house wasn't ready. Later - the house was ready and
      we did not want to wait.'
Pregnancies, of course, brought marriages forward - or even determined them. Two-fifths of those marrying in their teens said they got married when they did because they were pregnant. This proportion fell to 10% for those marrying in their twenties or thirties.

TIMING OF FIRST BIRTH

Twenty-one per cent of the mothers gave pregnancy as the reason for
getting married when they did, and 24% had a baby within eight
months of their marriage.   The interval between marriage and first
birth or pregnancy is shown in Table 22 for mothers marrying at
different ages. (If their first pregnancy ended in a miscarriage
or abortion, the interval between marriage and the time the pregnancy
would have ended if it had gone to term was calculated.   Ten per
cent ended in this way.)

TABLE 22   Age at marriage and interval between marriage and first
birth or pregnancy

Interval between marriage and first birth or pregnancy	Age at marriage				All mothers
	Under 20	20-24	25-29	30 or more	
	%	%	%	%	%
Before marriage*	3	2	2	5	3
Within 8 months of marriage	42	14	12	27	24
8 months < 1 year	13	14	18	18	14
1 year < 2 years	20	28	32	27	25
2 years < 3 years	11	17	21	10	15
3 years < 4 years	5	12	5	5	8
4 years < 5 years	2	7	2	5	5
5 years or longer	4	6	8	3	6
Number of mothers (=100%)	552	733	130	40	1,465

* But a child of both husband and wife.

Just over two-fifths of the mothers who married when they were in
their teens were pregnant at the time, and teenage marriages
accounted for 64% of the pre-nuptial conceptions.   Of those
marrying in their teens two-fifths would have preferred their first
pregnancy later - or would rather it had not happened at all, and
this proportion was two-thirds of those marrying in their teens
when they were pregnant.   Not all of these would necessarily have
wanted to postpone their marriage, but these data suggest that many
teenage marriages are timed or determined by unintended pregnancies.
   Less than half, 40%, of the first pregnancies to women in their
teens were said to be intended - and of course women who became
pregnant but did not marry the father were not included in the
survey.   Table 23 also shows that although nearly half the mothers
having their first pregnancy before they were twenty would have
preferred it later or were sorry it happened at all, less than a
fifth were using any method of birth control around the time they
became pregnant.

TABLE 23   Age at first pregnancy and mothers' intentions

	Age at first pregnancy				All first pregnancies
	Under 20	20-24	25-29	30 or more	
When first found pregnant felt:	%	%	%	%	%
Pleased	49	72	78	54	67
Rather earlier	3	8	12	40	10
Rather later	39	17	9	6	19
Sorry it happened at all	9	3	1	-	4
Used method of birth control around time pregnant:	%	%	%	%	%
Yes	17	17	7	3	14
No	83	83	93	97	86
Intended to become pregnant:	%	%	%	%	%
Yes	40	73	88	91	71
No	60	27	12	9	29
No. of mothers (=100%)*	129	290	153	35	610

* A small number for whom inadequate information was obtained have been excluded when calculating percentages.

The relationship between the timing of the first birth and mothers' feelings about the timing is shown in Table 24.

TABLE 24   Feelings about timing of the first birth

	Interval between marriage and first birth or pregnancy							
	Before marriage	Less than 8 months	8 mths < 1 yr	1 yr < 2yrs	2 yrs < 3 yrs	3 yrs < 4 yrs	4 yrs < 5 yrs	5 yrs or longer
	%	%	%	%	%	%	%	%
Right time	44	36	63	72	80	73	72	51
Preferred later	47	63	33	21	7	4	5	4
Preferred earlier	9	1	4	7	13	23	23	45
No. of mothers (=100%)	32	312	174	342	207	114	62	76

The most acceptable interval between marriage and the first baby would appear to be between two and three years. For shorter intervals between one-fifth and three-fifths of the mothers would have preferred the birth to be later, for longer intervals a fifth or more would have liked it earlier, and this proportion was nearly half of those who waited five years or more after they married before they had their first baby. However, for mothers who said they would have liked their first baby either earlier or later, the most frequently preferred time for both groups was between one and two years. This is shown in Table 25. It was also the most common interval for those who had their first baby when they wanted it.

TABLE 25   Preferred interval between marriage and first birth

Preferred interval for those who would have liked it to be different, actual interval for those who were happy with it:	Those preferring a shorter interval to the one they had	Those preferring a longer interval to the one they had	Those who had their first baby at the time wanted
	%	%	%
Less than a year	19	5	29
1 year < 2 years	40	48	30
2 years < 3 years	25	32	20
3 years < 4 years	10	9	10
4 years < 5 years	5	3	6
5 years or longer	1	3	5
No. of mothers (= 100%)	140	361	813

These data from Tables 24 and 25 suggest that while mothers who have their first baby between two and three years after they are married are the ones most satisfied with the timing of the birth, the interval most often perceived as being satisfactory is rather shorter - between one and two years.

When mothers were asked: 'Some people like to start a family straight away when they get married and others to leave it for a while, how did you feel about this?' 28% said they had favoured starting straight away, 64% leaving it for a while, and 8% made other comments. The reasons most commonly given, in order of their frequency, were first financial, by 26% of mothers, then, as a reason for leaving it a while, the need to 'get to know each other properly' or to 'have some time on our own before having children' - 23% of mothers said this. Eighteen per cent mentioned housing - 'we wanted to get a place of our own first.' Some of the reasons given for starting a family straight away were:

'You want to enjoy your children while you're young so the sooner you start your family the better really.'

'We decided to go for it right away because we feel we're getting on all right. If you start on it right away then you get it over with.'

'You can never tell if you are going to be able to have children.
You might wait a year and then find you couldn't have any.'
'I didn't like going to work - I just wanted a baby.'
'We both love children and we think that if you start having a
family when you're young you are still young when they are grown
up.'

Over half, 55%, of those marrying when they were pregnant would
have preferred to leave it a while, and this proportion did not vary
with the age at marriage.   Among those who were not pregnant when
they married, the proportion who said they had wanted to start a
family straight away was lowest among those marrying in their early
twenties.   It was 20% in this group compared with 30% of those
marrying in their teens and 35% of those marrying when they were 25
or more.   So a third of those marrying in their teens were keen to
take on the role of mother soon after they had taken on the role of
wife.

SPACE BETWEEN CHILDREN

Table 26 shows the interval between the last two children for all
mothers with two or more children and then for those mothers who
were happy with this interval.   ('Are you happy with the spacing you
have between the births of your - last two - children or would you
prefer it to be different?   IF PREFER DIFFERENT: 'What would you
like it to be?')   For mothers who would have preferred a different
interval Table 26 shows the space they would have liked between
their last two children.   Finally the preferred interval before the
next child is shown in the last column for mothers who hoped to have
another child.   ('How long a time would you like to have between the
last baby and the next one - that is between the two births?'   Those
who were already pregnant were asked about the interval they would
have liked to have.)

TABLE 26   Interval between children

	Actual interval between last two children		Preferred interval between last two for mothers who were not happy with it	Preferred interval before next
	All mothers with two or more children	Mothers who were happy with the interval		
	%	%	%	%
Less than a year	2	2	2	2
1 year < 1½ years	14	16	9	9
1½ yrs < 2 years	15	17	32	26
2 years < 3 years	28	34	42	38
3 years < 4 years	16	14	10	15
4 years < 5 years	9	6	4	6
5 years < 6 years	5	4	1	3
6 years < 7 years	3	2	-	-
7 years or longer	8	5	-	1
No. of mothers (= 100%)	807	582	212	755

Half or more of the preferred or liked intervals were between one and a half but less than three years, and almost nine-tenths of the preferred intervals were between one year but less than four years. But just over a quarter, 27%, of the actual intervals between the last two births fell outside this range, most of them being longer. Mothers were more likely to regret pregnancies which happened after a longer interval.   The proportion who said they felt 'sorry it happened at all' rose from 15% of those occurring after an interval of less than three years to 30% after an interval of four to six years and 43% after seven years or longer.

The mothers' feelings about the interval between their last two children, and the way this varied with the actual interval, are shown in Table 27.

TABLE 27   Attitude to interval between last two children

	Interval between last two children						All mothers with two or more children
	Less than 1½ yrs	1½ yrs <2 yrs	2 yrs <3 yrs	3 yrs <4 yrs	4 yrs <5 yrs	5 yrs +	
	%	%	%	%	%	%	%
Prefer shorter	1	2	8	33	49	46	19
Happy with it	75	87	89	65	51	54	74
Prefer longer	24	11	3	2	-	-	7
No. of mothers (=100%)	134	115	225	129	68	119	790

More mothers would have liked the children to be closer together than would have preferred them further apart.

The way intervals varied for different birth orders is shown in Table 28.   With third or later born children an interval of five or more years is more common than it is between first and second births.

TABLE 28   Family size and space between last two children

	Number of children			
	Two	Three	Four	Five or more
	%	%	%	%
Less than 2 years	36	24	21	32
2 years < 3 years	33	24	21	17
3 years < 5 years	22	28	38	21
5 years or longer	9	24	20	30
No. of mothers (=100%)	469	208	76	53

A rather similar pattern is found in Table 29, which shows the preferred interval before the next birth for mothers who wanted further children.   Four-fifths of those wanting a second child hoped to have it within three years compared with just over half of those wanting a third child.   Variation was greatest among those looking forward to a fourth or later birth, with two-fifths wanting it within two years and just over a fifth intending to wait for four years or longer.

TABLE 29 Family size and preferred interval before next birth

	Present family size		
	One	Two	Three or more
	%	%	%
Less than 1½ years	11	7	13
1½ years < 2 years	30	14	28
2 years < 3 years	41	32	29
3 years < 4 years	13	23	8
4 years < 5 years	3	12	10
5 years or longer	2	12	12
Number of mothers wanting further children (= 100%)	529	172	52

When asked how they felt in general terms about having children close together or having a longer time between them, two-thirds of the mothers said they preferred to have them close together, a fifth liked them further apart, and the rest made other comments. ('Some people like to have their children close together and others prefer to have a longer time between them.   What do you feel about this?')   The main reason given for preferring a shorter birth interval mentioned by 56% of all mothers was the better relationship between children.
'They grow up together and are company for each other.'
Only 1% thought the relationship between children was better if there was a longer interval.   Nine per cent mentioned the practical advantage of looking after children near in age.
'So that you don't put the nappies away and then have to start again.'
'I like to have all the hard work at one time.'
And 8% that they wanted to get child rearing over with.
'Otherwise you've never finished - you're still looking after children when you're old.'
'I don't want to go on for years and years having children.
I'd like to go back to work.'
Among the reasons for preferring a longer birth interval, 20% of all mothers felt this would enable them to look after children better and give them more time, attention, and love.   Six per cent felt a longer interval gave the first child a better chance to get more established physically and emotionally before the next child,

while 1% thought the emotional reaction of the older child was
likely to be better if there was a relatively short gap.   Five per
cent preferred a longer interval for the mother to recover.

'It gives you time to get on your feet physically and mentally
from one baby before you start again.   It's a hard job bringing
up small children.'

The proportion who said they preferred them closer together fell
from 80% of those whose last interval had been less than two years
to 45% of those whose last children had between five and six years
between them, then rose to 70% for those with a longer interval of
seven years or longer - presumably a reflection of the fact that
many of the mothers with such an interval between births had not
chosen it deliberately.   Although actual spacing was related to
their views, the association could arise because people tend to
like what they have rather than because many plan their families
to fit in with their ideas of appropriate birth intervals.   But
as suggested earlier (in Chapter 2) it would seem that spaces
between children are related to parents' desire for further
children.   This is indicated by the data in Table 30.

TABLE 30   Hopes for more children and space between last two

Space between last two:	Proportion wanting more or pregnant now		
	2 children in family	3 children in family	4 or more children in family
Less than eighteen months	30% (86)	25% (28)	15%} (33)
1½ years < 2 years	32% (81)	10% (21)	
2 years < 3 years	14% (153)	6% (49)	0% (25)
3 years < 4 years	17% (71)	3% (36)	5% (20)
4 years < 5 years	13% (31)	10% (20)	4%} (27)
5 years < 7 years	16% (25)	15% (26)	
7 years or longer	5% (20)	0% (25)	0% (22)

Numbers in brackets are figures on which percentages are based
(= 100%)

It might be thought that mothers who have had two babies in
quick succession might be less inclined than mothers who had spaced
their children more widely to want another child.   The data in
Table 30 refute this and suggest that mothers who want further
children space their children more closely together than mothers
who do not.

IMPLICATIONS

One clear implication of the high proportion of unintended teenage
pregnancies is that many of these would be avoided if more teenagers
were using effective contraception.

Doubtless many of these births to teenage mothers would simply
be postponed if unintended pregnancies were reduced, but there is

some evidence that women who have their first pregnancy in their
teens have more children on average than those who start their
childbearing later, and they are of course at risk to subsequent
pregnancies for a longer period. The relationship between age at
first pregnancy and family size on this study is shown in Table 31.

TABLE 31 Family size and age at first pregnancy

	Age at first pregnancy			
	Under 20	20-24	25-29	30 or more
Average number of children:				
At time of interview	2.14	2.00	1.67	1.61
At time of interview by those not wanting more	2.68	2.59	2.24	2.15
Wanted altogether by those wanting more or uncertain	2.79	2.64	2.43	2.39
Intended*	2.74	2.62	2.34	2.30
Number of mothers on which averages based				
Not wanting more	167	348	130	26
Wanting more or uncertain	182	373	169	38
Total number of mothers	355	736	305	64

* That is the present number for those who did not want further
children and the number wanted altogether by those who did or
were uncertain.

   Among those not wanting more, mothers having their first
pregnancy in their teens already had an average of over half a
baby more than those who waited until the second half of their
twenties before becoming pregnant, while among those wanting further
children the difference between these two groups in the number
wanted amounted to about a third of a child on average.
 There is a challenge to contraceptive services and health education.
In 1973 there were over 42,000 legitimate first births to mothers
under 20 and this study suggests that 60% of them, around 25,000,
were unintended. There were in addition nearly 21,000 illegitimate
maternities among women under 20, of which probably a larger
proportion were unintended, and 26,500 abortions to women of that
age (Office of Population Censuses and Surveys, 1975, Tables,
Population and 1974c).
   The next few chapters are concerned with the ways in which
people control or fail to control their fertility, their use of
contraception and contraceptive services, and the attitudes to
different methods of birth control, including abortion.

Part one

CONTROLLING FERTILITY

Chapter 5

USE OF CONTRACEPTION

Nearly all the mothers, 97%, had used a method of birth control at some time but nevertheless a third of their most recent pregnancies, leading to the survey baby, were said to be unintended.   In an attempt to identify some of the attributes of mothers likely to become pregnant when they do not want to be, this chapter looks first at some of the characteristics of mothers using different methods of contraception.

RELIGION AND ATTITUDES TO BIRTH CONTROL

Two per cent of the mothers disapproved of the idea of birth control, 87% were in favour and 11% had mixed feelings.   ('Many people do something to limit the number of children they have or to control the time when they have them.   In general, would you say you are for this or against this, or have you got mixed feelings?')   In 1967/68 rather more mothers, 6%, had been against it.   In both studies this attitude was related to religion.
    Almost two-thirds, 64%, of the mothers in the current study described themselves as Church of England, 13% as other Protestants, 13% as Catholics, 2% as Moslems, 1% as Hindu, 3% as having some other religion, and 4% as being Atheists, Agnostics, or having no religion.   ('What is your religion, if any?')   The Catholics were slightly less likely than the Protestants to say they were in favour of birth control, 81% against 88%, but it was the Moslems who were least likely to approve of it, just over half, 54%, of them did so. Even so, over half of those who were against it were Church of England or other Protestants, a fifth were Catholics, and a fifth Moslems.
    The small proportion of mothers, 2%, who were against birth control presented the most extreme picture in terms of their use of contraception.   Over half of them were not using any method of birth control, a quarter were using withdrawal, two of the 29 had been sterilized themselves, one husband had had a vasectomy, one was using the sheath, none were using the pill, cap, coil, or, more surprisingly, the safe period or abstinence.
    The differences between Catholic and other mothers in their

current use of birth control methods were relatively small.   Rather
more of the Catholics were not using any method of birth control,
18% compared with 9%;   more of them relied on the safe period, 4%
against 1%; and fewer of their husbands had been sterilized, 1%
compared with 4%.   There were no significant differences in their
current use of the pill, coil, withdrawal, and female sterilization.
The same differences, or lack of differences, emerge if Catholics
are compared with just Church of England and Protestant mothers.
(Ryder and Westoff also found 'the fact of being Catholic is
becoming less significant as a factor in shaping attitudes toward
fertility and...in the practice of contraception itself.' See
Ryder and Westoff, 1971, p.102.)
    When the proportions who had ever used different methods of
birth control are considered, there are more differences between
Catholics and Protestants.   Fewer Catholics had ever taken the
pill - 57% against 68%, and fewer had used the sheath - 58% against
72%.
    The differences between Moslems and others were greater.   Nearly
half, 46%, of them, 10% of others, were currently using nothing at
all and relatively few of the Moslem mothers were taking the pill,
23% compared with 43%, or using the sheath, 8% against 22%.   There
was a greater degree of endogamy among the Moslems than the
Catholics;   all the Moslem mothers had Moslem husbands, 48% of
Catholic mothers had Catholic husbands.
    The Moslem mothers intended to have the largest families - an
average of 3.90 compared with 2.56 for others.   Catholics 'wanted'
an average of 2.76.
    It may, of course, be that a lower use of birth control influenced
expectations and ambitions.   The relationship with family size and
hopes for further children is looked at next.

HOPES FOR FURTHER CHILDREN AND FAMILY SIZE

Use of different methods of birth control was related to their hopes
or otherwise for further children.   This can be seen from Table 32.
The picture is complicated by sterlization as those who have been
sterilized are not in a position to change their minds about having
further children.   Use of the pill or sterilization, the two most
reliable methods, increased from 45% of those who hoped for more
children to 59% of those who did not and said they would not change
their minds.   If the cap, coil, and sheath are included as being
relatively reliable, the proportion rises from 76% to 86%.
    When those who did not want more children were asked how they
would feel if they found they were pregnant (only mothers who did
not want more children and had not been sterilized were asked this
question), there was no difference between those who said they
would feel 'very upset', 'fairly upset', or 'not upset' in the
methods of birth control they were currently using.   But there
were clear differences between those using different methods in
their views on whether it was quite likely, rather unlikely or
very unlikely that they would become pregnant. These are shown in
Table 33.

TABLE 32   Variations in current use of different methods of birth control with hopes for more children

	Views on further children			
	Hopes for more	Uncertain	No - but might change mind	No and will not change mind
	%	%	%	%
Female sterilization	–	–	–	14
Male sterilization	– ⎫45	– ⎫49	– ⎫55	11 ⎫59
Pill	45 ⎭	49 ⎭	55 ⎭	34 ⎭
Cap	3	2	1	–
Coil	5	8	8	5
Sheath	23	18	22	22
Withdrawal	5	11	6	6
Safe period	2	4	1	1
Other	2 ⎫24	1 ⎫23	3 ⎫14	2 ⎫14
None	15 ⎭	7 ⎭	4 ⎭	5 ⎭
Number of mothers (=100%)	629	139	220	453

TABLE 33   Use of different methods of birth control and mothers' views on the likelihood of their becoming pregnant*

	Method currently used					
	Pill	Coil	Sheath	Withdrawal	Other	None
	%	%	%	%	%	%
Quite likely	4	2	12	26	5	34
Rather unlikely	29	34	42	37	50	14
Very unlikely	67	64	46	37	45	52
Number of mothers*	264	41	145	41	22	29

* Only mothers who did not want more children and had not been sterilized were asked this question.

A third of the mothers not using any method although they did not want more children recognized that they were quite likely to become pregnant, but half thought it very unlikely.   These mothers who did not want more children but were not using any method of contraception are a small but puzzling group.   There were thirty-

three of them altogether, and a third of them had never used any
method of contraception.   A number of these gave various reasons
why they did not think they would become pregnant.
   'I'm a worrier and when I worry nothing ever happens.   I
   couldn't fall pregnant with the second one as I was worrying
   about it.   The doctor suggested I should give up work and then
   I might feel more relaxed.   I did that and fell next month.'
   'We're not bothered by sex.   We haven't had it since the baby
   was born.   I don't mind.'
   'I must be too old now.   Peter must have been a real fluke.
   I'd had a scraping operation for heavy periods and then my
   periods had stopped and I haven't seen them since I had him.
   I didn't know I was having him till the day he was born.' (aged
   47 when last baby born)
Others seemed fatalistic or indifferent.
   'Children come when it's time.' (seven children)
   'I don't really know - I've never really bothered.' (one child)
   'We would never do any of those things - my husband laughs about
   them.'
One was already pregnant again.
   'I've always fallen before I could have anying.   I thought of
   having the coil but found I was pregnant.   Then I was going to
   be sterilized and found I was pregnant again.'
Some of those who had used some method in the past but were not
doing so around the time of interview also gave reasons why they
did not think they would become pregnant;   others expressed a
fatalistic view, but several gave reasons for not using or taking
a method they had used in the past.
   'I'm not allowed the pill and they won't fit the cap or the coil
   because I haemorrhage at my periods, and I don't like Durex -
   can't stand them, and we don't get on with the withdrawal method.
   I expect we shall try and use it though.'
   'The doctor has told me to stop (pill) as it didn't suit me -
   advised me to stop for two months.'
Among those not wanting any more children the proportion of mothers
who said they would feel very upset if they found they were pregnant
rose slightly from 27% of those who thought it quite likely they
would become pregnant to 33% of those who thought it rather unlikely
and 44% among those who felt it very unlikely - but as stated
earlier, the extent of anxiety about further children was not
directly related to the use of contraception.
   The proportion who would feel very upset did not vary significantly with the number of children they already had.   But there were
a number of differences in the methods of birth control used by
mothers with different sized families.   The proportion who had been
sterilized increased with family size.   This is shown in Table 34.
   A third of the mothers with five or more children had been
sterilized and the husbands of 15% had had a vasectomy, so half of
these couples could not have any more children.   In contrast, 4%
of those with two children could not do so - although two-fifths of
them said they did not want any more children and were certain they
would not change their minds.

TABLE 34 Variations in current use of different methods of birth control with size of family

	Number of children				
	One	Two	Three	Four	Five or more
	%	%	%	%	%
Female sterilization	-	2	10	21	34
Male sterilization	- ⎫ 47	2 ⎫ 53	7 ⎫ 52	17 ⎫ 59	15 ⎫ 62
Pill	47 ⎭	49 ⎭	35 ⎭	21 ⎭	13 ⎭
Cap	2	2	-	-	-
Coil	4	7	7	3	6
Sheath	24	21	22	20	6
Withdrawal	6 ⎫	6 ⎫	6 ⎫	8 ⎫	13 ⎫
Safe period	1 ⎬ 23	1 ⎬ 17	3 ⎬ 19	- ⎬ 18	2 ⎬ 26
Other	2 ⎪	2 ⎪	4 ⎪	1 ⎪	- ⎪
None	14 ⎭	8 ⎭	6 ⎭	9 ⎭	11 ⎭
No. of mothers (= 100%)	607	497	218	76	53

While use of the pill went down with increasing family size, this was more than offset by sterilization, so that use of these two most reliable methods went up from 47% to 62% with increasing family size. A rather different pattern was found with age.

AGE

Sterilization and use of the pill were strongly related to age, but in opposite directions. And the proportion using one or other of these fell from three-fifths of those under 20 to two-fifths of those aged 30 or more. This can be seen from Table 35.

Older mothers were not only less likely than younger ones to be currently taking the pill, they were less likely to have ever taken it and more likely to have given it up if they had tried it. The proportion who had ever taken it fell from 73% of mothers under 20 to 34% of those aged 35 or more, and the proportion of those who had tried it but were no longer taking it rose from 17% to 69%. Yet older women were more at risk to an unwanted pregnancy; relatively few of them, 9% of those aged 35 or more, wanted another baby and the proportion who had felt 'sorry it happened at all' about their last pregnancy was 24% among those aged 30-34 and 35% for those aged 35 or more compared with 10% of younger mothers.

Mothers may feel, quite rightly, that they are less likely to become pregnant as they get older, but an unintended pregnancy may be a more disturbing event for them. There has been a great deal of emphasis recently on contraceptive services for younger age groups, and the needs of older women may have been somewhat over-looked.

TABLE 35   Age and current use of different methods of birth control

	Age				
	Under 20	20-24	25-29	30-34	35 or over
	%	%	%	%	%
Female sterilization	-	1	5	10	20
Male sterilization	}62	2 }55	4 }50	6 }39	11 }42
Pill	62	52	41	23	11
Cap	-	1	3	2	1
Coil	2	5	8	7	4
Sheath	15	20	24	24	25
Withdrawal	3	6	6	9	9
Safe period	1 }21	1 }19	1 }15	3 }28	2 }28
Other	1	2	2	1	3
None	16	10	6	15	14
No. of mothers (=100%)	144	540	480	198	85

FREQUENCY OF INTERCOURSE

It has been suggested that women having intercourse relatively frequenly are more likely to be taking the pill than women who have it less often.   In this study the average reported frequency of intercourse in the week before interview was 2.01 for mothers taking the pill compared with 1.74 for other mothers - a significant difference.   ('Have you and your husband had intercourse in the last seven days?' IF YES 'How many times?' The distribution of replies is shown on p. 88.)   But pill taking is more common and intercourse more frequent among younger women.   When age was taken into account there were no significant differences, but this is different from the findings in another study (Ryder and Westoff, 1971, pp.173-4).

SOCIAL CLASS (For a description of the classification of Social Class see Appendix II.)

Social class variations in the methods currently used are shown in Table 36.   Those that stand out in relation to taking the pill are the wives of men in professional occupations.   Only 31% of them were taking the pill compared with 40% or more of mothers in the other groups.   However, if the proportions who had ever taken the pill are compared, there is a trend from 69% of those in Social Class I down to 59% in Social Class V.   In 1967/68 too, more of those in Social Class I than of the other mothers had taken the pill at some time.   They appear to have been the first to try it but also the first to give it up.   A study in Finland found similar results and argued that:

the use of the pill is no exception to the general rule that innovations are first adopted by the well-to-do and better educated strata, and spread gradually to other social groups... It could be hypothesized that the upper strata...also have been the first ones to discontinue its use because of the widely publicised and discussed health hazards of oral contraceptives (Leppo et al., 1973-4).

TABLE 36   Variations in current use of different methods of birth control with social class

	I	II	III Skilled		IV	V
			N	M		
	%	%	%	%	%	%
Female sterilization	3	5	3	4	5	7
Male sterilization	-	2	2	4	6	3
Pill	31	40	46	45	41	43
Cap	4	3	4	1	-	1
Coil	9	8	5	5	5	4
Sheath	30	25	24	21	21	15
Withdrawal	1 ⎫	5 ⎫	6 ⎫	7 ⎫	9 ⎫	7 ⎫
Safe period	8 ⎬ 23	1 ⎬ 17	2 ⎬ 16	1 ⎬ 20	- ⎬ 22	1 ⎬ 27
Other	-	2	1	2	1	4
None	14 ⎭	9 ⎭	7 ⎭	10 ⎭	12 ⎭	15 ⎭
No. of mothers (= 100%)	93	197	131	608	247	116

Other differences were a trend for the sheath to be used more by the middle-class and less by working-class mothers, and a trend in the opposite direction for withdrawal.   Both these differences were also observed on the 1967/68 study and, more surprisingly, on both studies more of the middle- than of the working-class mothers reported use of the safe period.   The other difference between middle- and working-class mothers in the recent study is the greater prevalence of male sterilization among the working- than among the middle-class, 4% compared with 1%.

PAST EXPERIENCE OF CONTRACEPTION

Mothers had tried an average of 2.31 different methods of contraception - including the one they were currently using.   As might be expected, older mothers had tried rather more methods than younger ones, but the difference was not great: an average of 2.23 for mothers under 25 compared with 2.40 for mothers aged 25 or more. There was much more variation between mothers currently using

different methods.   Those who had been sterilized had tried the
largest number of methods - an average of 3.22, then those with a
coil 2.91, and those using a cap 2.68.   Those taking the pill had
tried an average of 2.33, while those using the sheath and withdrawal
were the least likely to have tried other methods - an average of
2.12 and 1.98.

The proportions of those who had ever tried different methods who
had given them up are shown in Table 37.

TABLE 37   Proportion who had given up different methods of
contraception

	Proportion who had given method up	Number who had ever tried method (= 100%)
Pill	34%	956
Cap	83%	145
Coil	29%	116
Sheath	67%	1013
Withdrawal	83%	652
Safe period	79%	190
Chemicals	82%	110
Abstinence	85%	71

Abstinence, the cap, withdrawal, spermicides, and the safe period
all had 'rejection rates' of more than three-quarters.   The pill
and coil had the lowest rejection rates but, as can be seen from
Table 38, four-fifths of the mothers with a coil had only tried that
method since the last survey baby was born.   Withdrawal, the cap,
and the sheath had been used for five or more years by about a third
of the mothers currently using those methods.

TABLE 38   Length of time for which current method of contraception
had been used

	Current method of contraception					
	Pill	Cap	Coil	Sheath	Withdrawal	Safe period
	%	%	%	%	%	%
Since last baby	44	19	82	33	25	28
1 year < 2 years	6	14	1	8	7	19
2 years < 3 years	15	5	6	11	9	10
3 years < 4 years	10	19	4	12	16	14
4 years < 5 years	10	10	2	7	11	5
5 years < 10 years	14	33	5	23	16	5
10 years or more ago	1	-	-	6	16	19
Number	625	21	81	315	92	21

What effect does a contraceptive failure have on their subsequent
use of birth control?   Just over a fifth of the mothers said they
had conceived the study baby while they were attempting some form of
birth control.   Nearly half, 46%, of the 'accidents' occurred with
the sheath, a third, 31%, with withdrawal, a tenth with the safe
period.   The reason for the accident, in terms of the mothers'
perceptions of it ('Do you think it happened because you didn't
always take/use it - you didn't always use it properly - or the
method was unreliable?'), varied with the different methods, as can
be seen from Table 39.

TABLE 39 Mothers' perceptions of reasons for contraceptive failure

	Pill	Cap or chemicals	Sheath	With-drawal	Safe period	All methods*
	%	%	%	%	%	%
Did not always use method	56	60	63	16	13	44
Did not use properly	9	16	9	22	40	16
Method unreliable	35	24	28	62	47	40
Number of pregnancies	23	25	141	92	32	308

* Includes IUD - all five failures for which were regarded as the
  method unreliable.

Most of the pill, sheath, and cap or spermicide failures arose
because the mothers did not always use them.   Failures of withdrawal
were more usually attributed to the method being unreliable.   Seventy
per cent of those who had had a pill failure were taking the pill
around the time of interview.   Comparable proportions for the sheath
were 30%, withdrawal 21%, and the safe period 6%.   Comparisons with
current use for all mothers show there was a tendency for people to
persist with the same method in spite of failure.   And mothers who
had experienced a failure seemed as likely as other mothers to 'take
a chance' with the methods they were currently using.   One in eight
of the mothers said they sometimes took a chance with the method
they were currently relying on and did not always use or take it.
(IF PILL 'Do you take it every day or sometimes miss?'   IF OTHER
METHODS (APART FROM IUD OR STERILIZATION) 'Do you always use it - one -
or sometimes take a chance?')   The proportion taking chances was
lower among pill-takers, 10%, than for those using other method, 15%.

POSSIBLE CHANGES IN THE FUTURE

The 11% of mothers who were not using any method of birth control
were asked if they thought they would use something in the future.
Of these, 16% said they would not do so, and another 11% were
uncertain.   The methods they thought they were most likely to use

were fairly similar to the current pattern of use among other
mothers - the pill being most frequently mentioned, by 35%, sterilization by 13%, the sheath by 13%, and the coil by 10%.

Those currently using a method were asked about possible changes
in the future. ('Do you think you are likely to change some time
and use a different method - from the one you are using now - ever?)
Replies are in Table 40 analysed by the method they were using
around the time of interview.

TABLE 40   Possible changes in the use of contraceptive methods

	Current method							All mothers using method*
	Pill	Cap	Coil	Sheath	With-drawal	Safe period	Other	
	%	%	%	%	%	%	%	%
Unlikely to change	55	32	65	34	25	38	15	51
Might change to:								
Male sterilization	11	5	14	10	6	5	22	10
Female sterilization	8	5	9	4	6	5	11	6
Pill	-	23	11	33	33	33	30	13
Coil	14	27	-	15	23	5	15	13
Sheath	7	-	2	-	2	5	7	4
Other, incl. cap	5	-	1	4	5	14	4	4
New method	2	5	1	1	1	5	4	1
Uncertain	3	5	2	4	4	-	4	3
No. of mothers (= 100%)**	627	22	81	317	93	21	27	1,301

*   Including mothers who had been sterilized or those whose husbands
had been sterilized.
** Percentages add to more than 100 as some mothers gave more than
one answer.

Those least likely to say they might change were those using the
coil or taking the pill.   Even so, a third of those with a coil and
nearly half of those taking the pill thought they might do so.
Around two-thirds of those using the cap, sheath, or the safe period
thought they might change, and three-quarters of those using withdrawal.   Altogether half the mothers did not think they would
change - but the other half thought they might do so.

Older mothers of 30 or more were less likely than younger mothers
to predict a change, 43% against 52% said they might make one.
This difference arose because of the smaller proportion of older
women who thought they might try the pill - 9% compared with 15%.

Although many of the individual mothers may change their method of contraception, the main changes that seem likely to result in the general pattern of contraceptive use are an increase in the proportion sterilized and an increase in the proportion using the coil.   There might be a small decrease in the proportion taking the pill, but larger ones in the proportion using the sheath and other methods.   The possible change in patterns is shown in Table 41.

TABLE 41 Possible changes in the pattern of use of different contraceptive methods

	Present use	Possible future use
	%	%
Female sterilization	4	11
Male sterilization	3	13
Pill	43	38
Coil	6	16
Sheath	23	12
Cap	2 ⎫	
Withdrawal	8 ⎬ 15	7
Safe period	3 ⎪	
Other	2 ⎭	
None	11	3
Number of mothers * (=100%)	1,457	

* Percentages can add to more than 100 as some mothers mentioned more than one method.

The possible changes should probably be regarded as the maximum ones likely, as the estimate is based on the assumption that all those who said they might change do so.   Many of the reasons given for a change reflect the attributes they value in a contraceptive. Comments concerned with reliability were:
'Once I have had the number of children I want I will want to use a safer method - one that is 100% safe.' (using sheath, will probably change to coil)
'If I fell for another baby quickly I might change to the pill but I am sure happy with withdrawal at the moment.'
Experience of side effects and anxieties about health hazards and long-term consequences came up in many comments about the pill:
'I shall persevere with the pill for a while longer - and if I still have break-throughs and am still off intercourse then the doctor will fit the coil.'
'I was thinking once my periods become right - to revert to the pill - and a vasectomy maybe in several years' time. It's wiser not to stay on the pill indefinitely.' (using sheath)
'There's various comments you hear about it.   Rather than take the pill every day until I'm 50 I'd rather be sterilized.'
Others were concerned about sexual pleasure.
'Because my husband would enjoy sex much more and I admit I

would too - because there's no messing about in the middle.'
(using sheath - will change to pill but has not done so already
because breast-feeding)
'We don't like them - it spoils the enjoyment.' (using chemicals,
waiting to be fitted with coil)
A number of comments related to the services - or their perceptions
of them.
'The coil after I've had my second baby - you can't use it
before.'
'My husband will most likely be done if it becomes free for men
to have a vasectomy.'
'They say you should have a break of three months once a year
(from the pill) to get it out of your system.'
'Only if one of us is sterilized. It costs about £45.   If it
would be free one of us would do it.'
Attitudes to different methods of birth control and mothers'
views and experience of contraceptive services are discussed in more
detail in the next two chapters.

Chapter 6

ATTITUDES TO DIFFERENT METHODS OF BIRTH CONTROL

This chapter starts with an assessment of different methods of
contraception by the mothers currently using them.   This suggests
that the pill, the IUD, and sterilization were underused in that
more couples regarded them as satisfactory methods of birth control
than were currently using them.   Possible reasons for this are
explored for each of the three methods in turn.   Finally mothers'
views on abortion are discussed.

ASSESSMENT OF DIFFERENT METHODS OF CONTRACEPTION

In the previous chapter it was shown that the main reasons why
mothers contemplated a change in their contraception were the
relative reliability, health hazards, and pleasantness to use of
the different methods.   Their assessments of the method they were
currently using according to these three attributes are shown in
Table 42.   In addition mothers were asked for an overall assessment
of the method they were using.   ('Would you describe ---------
-method using now - on balance as a very satisfactory method, a
fairly satisfactory method, a rather unsatisfactory method or a very
unsatisfactory method?')
     Sterilization and then the pill were appropriately regarded as
the most reliable methods of contraception, the safe period and
withdrawal as the least so.   The pill and withdrawal were the ones
most often thought to involve a health risk.   Nearly all those who
thought withdrawal was not quite safe to use from the point of view
of health felt it was 'bad psychologically'.   The main ways in
which the pill was seen as a possible health hazard were first that
it might cause thrombosis or blood clots - 11% of all pill-users
mentioned that.   Their other main concern, mentioned by 9%, was
the possible long-term effects.
     'Not enough research into long-term effects.'
     'I don't think it's a good method to stay on too long.   I think
18 months at a time is long enough.'
     'I wouldn't like the thought of staying on it for 25 years.   We
take enough chemicals and artificial things into our bodies - in
foods and medicines.   I don't mind taking it for five years but
not for the rest of the time I have periods.'

TABLE 42 Views of different methods of contraception among mothers currently using them*

Assessment of current method	Mothers currently using:							
	Pill	Cap	IUD	Sheath	With-draw-al	Safe period	Female Steri-liza-tion	Male Steri-liza-tion
	%	%	%	%	%	%	%	%
Reliability								
Very	83	78	54	40	22	31	91	98
Fairly	15	22	45	53	42	46	6	2
Not very	2	–	1	7	36	23	3	–
Health hazards	%	%	%	%	%	%	%	%
Safe for health	70	96	87	97	74	100	95	96
Not safe or uncertain	30	4	13	3	26	–	5	4
Pleasant and easy to use	%	%	%	%	%	%	%	%
Yes	97	44	95	65	67	92	98	95
No	3	26	4	31	29	4	2	–
Other comment	–	30	1	4	4	4	–	5
On balance	%	%	%	%	%	%	%	%
Very satisfactory	77	36	72	31	19	37	89	100
Fairly satis-factory	21	55	25	57	49	52	11	–
Rather unsatis-factory	2	9	–	10	27	11	–	–
Very unsatis-factory	–	–	1	2	4	–	–	–
Other	–	–	2	–	1	–	–	–
No. of mothers currently using method (=100%)**	673	23	84	370	114	27	69	49

* A few mothers, 8%, who were not currently using a method were asked about the one they had used most recently and 1%, who had never used a method, about the one they were most likely to use.
** Small numbers for whom inadequate information was obtained have been omitted when calculating the percentages.

TABLE 43 Methods of birth control thought to be better than method currently using

	Mothers currently using							
	Pill	Cap	IUD	Sheath	With-draw-al	Safe period	Female sterili-za-tion	Male sterili-za-tion
More reliable	%	%	%	%	%	%	%	%
None	42	13	10	9	9	-	91	93
Female ⎤ steril-	38	26	37	35	31	48	-	2
Male ⎬ ization	41	30	32	38	29	48	5	-
Unspec.⎦	2	4	-	1	1	4	-	-
Pill	-	74	75	68	62	81	3	-
Cap	1	-	-	6	12	19	-	-
IUD	7	13	-	17	24	44	-	-
Sheath	1	-	1	-	13	19	-	-
Others	7	-	8	11	6	30	-	4
Uncertain	3	4	1	4	7	7	2	-
More pleasant and easy to use	%	%	%	%	%	%	%	%
None	82	13	50	20	29	48	89	95
Female ⎤ steril-	8	4	13	14	10	4	-	-
Male ⎬ ization	10	4	12	18	12	7	5	-
Unspec.⎦	1	-	-	2	-	-	-	-
Pill	-	83	33	61	41	44	2	2
Cap	-	-	-	1	3	-	-	-
IUD	3	26	-	13	12	11	-	-
Sheath	-	-	1	-	7	-	3	-
Others	-	-	-	2	-	-	-	-
Uncertain	2	-	4	4	7	4	2	2
More satisfactory on balance	%	%	%	%	%	%	%	%
None	70	30	55	27	20	48	89	98
Female ⎤ steril-	14	-	13	14	15	7	-	2
Male ⎬ ization	18	4	11	19	18	7	3	-
Unspec.⎦	1	-	1	1	1	-	-	-
Pill	-	61	29	52	48	41	5	-
Cap	1	-	-	2	4	11	-	-
IUD	5	13	-	13	19	26	-	-
Sheath	-	-	-	-	5	4	-	-
Others	1	-	-	2	2	4	-	-
Uncertain	2	-	4	4	5	7	3	-
No. of mothers (= 100%)*	673	23	84	370	114	27	69	49

* Some percentages add to more than 100 as some mothers gave more than one answer.

As far as ease and pleasantness of use were concerned, sterilization, the pill, the coil, and the safe period were all highly regarded by over nine-tenths of their users. The sheath and withdrawal were thought to be pleasant and easy to use by two-thirds of their users, the cap by a small proportion.

When asked to sum up their views and say on balance how satisfactory they felt the method they were using was, the relative ranking was first sterilization, second the pill, thirdly the coil. These three methods were all thought to be 'very satisfactory' by at least seven out of ten of the mothers using them. None of the other methods were anything like as satisfactory. The cap and safe period tied for fourth place - just over one in three of the users found them very satisfactory. The sheath came sixth and withdrawal well behind in seventh place.

Of course the people not using a method may have very different views about it from the people who are using it. Mothers were asked if they thought any method was more satisfactory than the one they were currently using. Table 43 shows their replies. The pill is regarded as a more reliable method by three-fifths or more of women using the cap, IUD, sheath, withdrawal, and the safe period. It is also thought to be more pleasant and easy to use by a third or more of such women. When their general views are considered it would seem surprising that the pill, IUD, and sterilization are not more widely used, while the sheath and withdrawal are used by as many couples. One plausible explanation would seem to be the availability or acceptability of services. The pill, IUD, and sterilization all depend on medical help, the sheath and withdrawal do not.

THE PILL

The pill was generally seen as a reliable method of contraception which is pleasant and easy to use. One possible reason why more people do not use the pill is that it is 'too reliable' for any who prefer to have some chance of becoming pregnant. In an attempt to identify any such mothers they were all asked: 'Other things being equal, would you prefer a method to be absolutely 100% reliable or to have a small chance of failure?' Seven per cent of the mothers opted for a slight risk. This group contained a relatively small proportion of mothers who had been sterilized (or whose husbands had been sterilized), 3% compared with 8% of

those wanting a method to be 100% reliable.   The other difference
was that more of those preferring an element of risk were using the
safe period, 7% compared with 1%, so a few may be playing a contraceptive version of Russian roulette quite deliberately.   But there
was no significant difference in the two groups in the proportion
taking the pill.

The main disadvantages of the pill are the health risks associated
with it and that it can only be obtained on a doctor's prescription.
The reasons given by mothers for not taking the pill although they
regarded it as more reliable or more pleasant and easy to use or
more satisfactory than the method they were using were general
worries about health and side effects (49%), actual experience of
side effects (22%), and a doctor advising them not to take it (13%).
Altogether health risks were mentioned by four-fifths.   Four per
cent mentioned the problems of getting it or said they had not got
round to getting it, 3% difficulties remembering to take it, and
1% the expense.   Older mothers of 30 or more were more likely to
mention health risks as a reason for not taking the pill than
younger mothers, 87% against 78%.   It can be argued that the
differences in age in the proportions currently taking the pill are
a generation rather than an age effect.   People who started using
contraception after the pill was available may well be prepared to
accept it more readily than those for whom it was an innovation
introduced only after they had started to use another method.   It
is not surprising if the present generation of older mothers regard
it more suspiciously than the younger mothers who are more likely
to accept such a method of contraception.   As this generation of
mothers grows older there is no reason why they should adopt the
views of older mothers about the pill, but how will their views
relate to their contraceptive practice?

There is a certain amount of evidence to suggest that many
women currently taking the pill may not be prepared to go on doing
so until the end of their reproductive life.   Among those who had
given up taking the pill, half said they had done so in order to
become pregnant, two-fifths because they had experienced side
effects, and 7% because of anxieties about possible effects.
Nearly two-thirds, 64%, of those who had ever taken the pill had
experienced some difficulties or problems which they thought were
caused by it.   ('Did or have you personally had any difficulties
or problems with it, or any symptoms you think were caused by it?')
The proportions still taking it were 83% of those who had not
experienced any side effects compared with 56% of those who
attributed some symptoms to it.   The symptoms most commonly
attributed to the pill were headaches, 19% of the women who had ever
taken the pill had had headaches which they thought were caused by
it, overweight - 16%, nausea - 14%, and depression - 13%.   These
are common symptom which many women are likely to experience.   (One
study found that 46% of a random sample of women aged 21 and over
reported headaches in a two-week period, 27% nerves, depression or
irritability, 14% a weight problem; Dunnell and Cartwright, 1972,
p.20.)   If they are taking the pill they may attribute the symptoms
to that and stop taking it.

If many mothers stop taking the pill, what methods of contra-

ception, if any, do they use instead?   Table 44 shows the methods
currently used by ex-pill-takers and those who had never taken the
pill.

TABLE 44   Methods of birth control currently used by ex-pill-takers
and others

	Ex-pill-takers	Never taken pill
	%	%
Female sterilization	11	6
Male sterilization	8	4
Cap	3	2
IUD	13	7
Sheath	36	41
Withdrawal	7	14
Safe period	2	3
Chemicals	3	1
Other	1	2
None	16	20
Number of mothers (= 100%)	323	507

One hypothesis was that people who had been on the pill would be
reluctant to use a coitus related method.   This appeared to be
borne out in that only 49% of ex-pill-takers were currently using
the cap, sheath, chemicals, and withdrawal compared with 58% of
mothers who had never taken the pill.   The individual methods
which differed in the two groups were sterilization and the IUD,
both of which were more commonly used by the ex-pill-takers, and
withdrawal which was used less often.   An alternative hypothesis
might be that ex-pill-users tend to use relatively reliable methods
of contraception.

THE IUD

Possible side effects, particularly heavy periods, was the most
common reason given for not having an IUD fitted by mothers who
thought it more reliable, easy to use, or generally more satisfactory than their current method.   A fifth mentioned this, 14%
the fear or dislike of either fitting, an internal examination,
the clinic, or the doctor.
   'I'm a coward and cringe at the thought of having one fitted.'
   'I suppose it's just the unpleasantness of going to have it
   fitted by the doctor - it's that more than anything else.'

Thirteen per cent thought it unreliable, 11% disliked the idea of
having something inside them.
  'I think it's alien to your body to have something inside you -
  unless it's a baby.'
  'I think basically it is bad, a mechanical device inside you
  inducing abortions every month.'
  'I've never fancied having anything inside me.'
Ten per cent said they did not know how to go about it, or enough
about it. 'I really don't know enough about it - I'd like to then
I might use it.'   Eight per cent had been advised against it by a
doctor.
  'The doctor suggested the coil but said it was likely to make
  you sterile - if you might change your mind about having another
  baby you'd be better on the pill.'
  'You've got to have two children before the doctors agree, I've
  been told at the clinic.'
  'The doctor advised against it.   I had actually made out to have
  it fitted at hospital when going for the post-natal.   I cancelled
  the appointment after seeing my G.P.'
Relatively few general practitioners, 12% in 1970/71, fitted IUD's,
and many had anxieties about associated health hazards - 57%
describing them as considerable or moderate (Cartwright and Waite,
1972).   Only a minority of family planning clinics in 1970, 39%,
fitted IUD's, and at these clinics women wanting an IUD would
probably have to wait a few weeks (Mitton, 1973).   So people
wanting an IUD needed knowledge, determination, and perseverance.

STERILIZATION

The main disadvantage about sterilization as a method of contraception is its irreversibility.   Mothers and fathers who had
mentioned either male or female sterilization as being more reliable,
safer for health, more pleasant or easy to use, or more satisfactory
on balance than the method they were currently using, were asked
why either they or their husbands or wives had not been sterilized.
Over two-thirds of both groups in both instances said it was because
it was too final, they might want more children.   This feelings
was strongly related to the mother's age, and to the number of
children she had.   The proportion of mothers who gave this reason
for not being sterilized fell from 94% of those with one child to
35% of those with four or more, and from 83% of those under 20 to
55% of those aged 35 or more.
  Among the others, inadequacy of services or unwillingness of
doctors to do the operation for them was sometimes a barrier.
Twelve mothers and 17 of their husbands were waiting for an
operation at the time of interview.   The cost of the operation was
deterring 21 of their husbands and 2 of the mothers from being
sterilized, and 17 mothers and 12 of their husbands had been refused
the operation.   So altogether, if services were more readily
available, data from the mothers suggest that a further 5% of
couples might be using sterilization compared with the 7% who were
doing so - a sizeable increase.   Information from the fathers gave
a similar proportion.

At a later question, mothers and fathers were asked if they would ever consider being sterilized.   Replies are shown in Table 45.

TABLE 45 Proportion of mothers and fathers who would consider being sterilized

	Mothers	Fathers
	%	%
Yes	36	42
Qualified or uncertain	17	15
No	47	43
Number of parents not sterilized = 100%	1,354	252

If anything, fathers seemed more prepared to consider being sterilized than mothers, but the difference might have arisen by chance.

Although the question asked whether they would ever consider it, there was a suggestion that some mothers may have taken a more short-term view since only 30% of those who wanted another child said they would ever consider it against 44% who definitely did not want another - the others falling in between.

In addition, analysis by age showed that the proportion of mothers who said they might ever consider being sterilized was comparatively low, 27%, among the under 20s.   If those who might consider it are added to those already sterilized or whose husbands had been sterilized, the proportion rises from 27% of those under 20 to 58% of those aged 35 or more.   But older men seemed more resistant to the idea than younger men.   The proportion who were not prepared to consider it at all was 58% of those aged 35 or more, compared with 39% of younger men.   This may be a generation effect.   For older women it appears a potentially popular method. It was also one that women not using any method of contraception were prepared to think about: as many of them as of other mothers, 36%, said they would consider being sterilized.

It is sometimes suggested that one reason why people are reluctant to consider sterilization as a form of birth control is that they think it will have an adverse effect on their sex life.

The most common view was that sterilization was unlikely to affect either a man's or a woman's sex life (see Table 46).   Among those who did not hold this view, rather more thought it would have a good rather than a bad effect.   This was particularly marked in relation to sterilization of women.   Reasons for feeling it would be better were mainly based on a single theme: 'Peace of mind.' 'More at ease not having to worry about becoming pregnant.' 'She can relax more and enjoy it as the risk of having a baby has gone.'

More of the mothers thought female sterilization was likely to improve a woman's sex life than male sterilization to improve a man's.   The difference in the proportion of fathers holding these two views might have occurred by chance and altogether there were

no significant differences between mothers and fathers in their
views on the effect of male or female sterilization on sex life.

TABLE 46   Views on likely effect of a sterilization on sex life*

	Likely effect on woman's sex life		Likely effect on man's sex life	
	Mothers	Fathers	Mothers	Fathers
Likely to make sex life	%	%	%	%
Better	28	23	17	18
Worse	8	12	11	13
No difference	47	41	56	53
Other comment	5	5	4	5
Don't know	12	19	12	11
Number of mothers or fathers (= 100%)	1,468	263	1,466	263

* 'Do you think sterilization of a woman/man is likely to make
her/his sex life better or worse or do you think it will not
make any difference?'

Some comments about the way in which sterilization might have a
bad effect on women were:
'Lose interest if you knew you couldn't conceive.'
'It can turn a woman funny. They haven't done enough research
on that. It's different for different women but it can make
them a bundle of nerves and go right off sex.'
'The risk that you might become pregnant would go - you would
lose some of the fire - wouldn't feel so feminine.'
And on men:
'They say it doesn't make him feel like a man and they lose
confidence in themselves.'
'Men like to think they're virile - got to be able to prove
that they're a man - they like to think they can have children.'
'They wouldn't feel as confident and they wouldn't get as much
enjoyment out of it - not enough risk involved.'
'It would break me - it's the ego more than anything. I
wouldn't like to think I couldn't father any more children.'
Views on the likely effect of sterilization on sex life were
clearly related to whether or not they would consider being sterilized themselves (see Table 47). But the association certainly
did not explain all the variation.
The views of mothers who had been sterilized, or whose husbands
had been sterilized, are shown in Table 48. Those with experience
were more likely to feel that sterilization had improved their own
or their husband's sex life. The one woman who had been sterilized
and thought it had made her sex life worse said:
'I'm not interested in sex at all now. I've no idea why but I'm
worse now than when I was on the pill. I wasn't very interested
on the pill but I'm even less interested now I've been doctored.'
Only seven of the fathers interviewed had been sterilized themselves.

Four of their wives had been sterilized.   None of those with
experience thought sterilization made sex life worse.

TABLE 47 Association between views on effect of sterilization on
sex life and whether would consider sterilization

	Mothers			Fathers		
	Thinks sterilization of woman likely to make sex life:			Thinks sterilization of man likely to make sex life:		
	Better	No effect	Worse	Better	No effect	Worse
Would consider being steril- ized	%	%	%	%	%	%
Yes	45	39	21	54	49	26
Qualified or uncertain	18	17	14	16	13	11
No	37	44	65	30	38	63
No. of mothers or fathers not sterilized	358	630	120	44	134	35

TABLE 48 Mothers' experience of sterilization and views on effect
of sterilization on sex life

Effect of sterilization on woman's sex life	Mother sterilized	Mother not sterilized
	%	%
Better	46	26
Worse	2	9
No difference	50	47
Other comment	2	5
Don't know	-	13
Number of mothers (= 100%)	64	1,404

Effect of sterilization on man's sex life	Husband sterilized	Husband not sterilized
	%	%
Better	52	16
Worse	-	12
No difference	48	55
Other comment	-	4
Don't know	-	13
Number of mothers (= 100%)	48	1,418

Taking the reported frequency of intercourse in the week before interview as an index of their sex life, mothers aged 30 or more who had been sterilized reported an average of 2.06 times against 1.23 for other mothers of that age.   This is different from findings in a survey in North America.   Westoff (1974) found that 'women with contraceptive sterlizations...report lower coital frequencies.'   (In this study mothers whose husbands had been sterilized reported an average of 1.55 but this did not differ significantly from other mothers of that age.)   Possibly mothers leading a relatively active sex life are more prepared to be sterilized.

In the previous chapter it was shown that sterilization was strongly related to age and from this one it is clear that older mothers are more interested in sterilization as a method of birth control.   Do parents feel that sterilization should be generally available to any man or woman who wants it - or should doctors only be prepared to do the operation under certain circumstances?   The proportion of mothers who thought that any woman ought to be able to get herself sterilized if she wanted it was 79%;   slightly more, 86%, thought that men ought to be able to have the operation if they wanted it.   Corresponding proportions for fathers were 70% thinking it should be generally available to women, 85% to men. So the paternalistic view was more widely held about female than male sterilization, and more common among fathers than mothers.

ABORTION

There was an even greater reluctance to leave the decision about abortion entirely to the woman concerned.   Rather less than half, 46%. of mothers and a similar proportion of fathers were apparently in favour of abortion on request, in that they thought any woman should be able to get an abortion if she wanted it.   A third held restrictive views, believing not only that any woman should not be able to get an abortion but also that a woman with several children should not necessarily be able to do so.   ('Do you think that any woman who finds she is pregnant when she does not want to be should be able to get an abortion - if she wants it?'   IF NO OR QUALIFIED 'If a woman who has several children finds she is pregnant when she does not want to be, do you think she should always be able to get an abortion if she wants it?')   The remaining fifth thought a woman with several children ought to be able to get an abortion but any woman who wanted one should not necessarily be able to do so. Altogether two-thirds of the mothers thought a woman with several children ought to be able to get an abortion if she wanted one. In the 1967/68 study only one-third thought this, and by 1970 the proportion was 37%.   This indicates a much greater acceptance of abortion in 1973. (Although the questions asked in the two surveys are directly comparable, the one in 1973 was preceded by the question about any woman.   This may have influenced responses to the question about a woman with several children.)

Those in favour of abortion on request made such comments as:
'If she wants it - everyone to their own opinion.   You must decide for yourself.'

Particular circumstances in which some thought it reasonable were
medical grounds (including if the child might be deformed) mentioned
by 20%, for financial reasons or if the mother had enough children
already - by 16%, if the baby was unwanted - by 10%, or if the mother
was unmarried, very young, or might otherwise be forced to marry,
3%.   Typical comments were:
   'If the baby is not wanted - if it's not going to be loved when
   it's born.'
   'Only for health reasons.'
   'Unless the child would have something wrong with it.'
   'If it would prevent a child being born who was spastic or
   mentally deformed.'
   'If they're poor and so on in some circumstances it would be
   better.'
   'If not married - or too many to cope with.'
Many of the reasons given against abortion were disapproving or even
punitive;
   'They should be more careful in the first place.'
   'It shouldn't be too easy - makes them more careless if they think
   abortions are easy to get.'
   'Well she could have it and then have a sterilization after.'
Almost a quarter, 23%, of the mothers made these types of comments.
Eleven per cent said they did not believe in it - for religious
reasons or because it was sinful.   And 9% referred to it as murder
or a crime.
   'It's a life.   It's killing.   I think it's murder.'
   'A lot of people have them in desperation and must suffer a lot
   afterwards thinking what they've done.   It must always be with
   you.   It's murder which ever way you look at it.'
Three per cent thought there was no need for abortion as the mother
could have the baby and then get it adopted.
   Attitudes to abortion did not vary significantly with social
class nor were they related to mothers' current use of different
contraceptive methods except that a relatively high proportion of
mothers using the cap were in favour of abortion on request, 73%
compared with 46% of other mothers.   Those with five or more
children were somewhat less liberal in their views, only 31% of
them thought any woman should be able to get an abortion compared
with 47% of those with smaller families.   At the same time more
of those who did not want any more children were in favour of
abortion on request than those who had not completed their families:
51% against 43%.
   With religion, those most antagonistic to abortion were the
Moslems, 65% were restrictive, then Catholics, 43%, Church of
England and other Protestants, 32%, and least opposed those with no
religion, 19%.   The proportion with restrictive views rose from
29% of those under 20 to 43% of those aged 35 or more.
   Mothers seemed less inclined to accept the idea of an abortion
for themselves than they were to tolerate others having one.   Twenty-
eight mothers, 1.9%, said they had had a previous pregnancy term-
inated by an abortion (24 of the 28 had been done by a doctor, 4
by someone else).   This compares with 17% who said they had had a
miscarriage and 2% a still birth.

Most of the married women who have abortions, three-quarters, do not want any more children (Cartwright and Lucas, 1974, p.27) so few of them would become eligible for this sample.   Half the women in this sample who had had abortions had them before they were married.

A larger number of mothers, 85, or 6%, had thought of trying to get an abortion when they found they were pregnant with the survey baby.   Two-thirds had discussed the possibility with a doctor.

One had initially been told that an abortion could be arranged but

'when it was confirmed that I was pregnant the doctor said it couldn't be done because I only had two children.   I don't think he asked anyone about it.   I think he told me yes in the first place until it was too late to do anything about it.'

Another had discussed it with her general practitioner and a psychiatrist at the hospital where she was having treatment.   She had gone to the general practitioner first, just a week after missing her period.

'I definitely didn't want the baby.   My reasons were financial and my mental condition.   The psychiatrist agreed that it would be unwise and gave me a note for my GP.   But she said it was rubbish - a definite no.   She believed every family should have more than one and I was being selfish to only want the one. She said the Committee were against it and they would not pass it.   She referred me to the physician, but she herself would not recommend it.   Well, he was more sympathetic but he couldn't - he'd have to refer me to another specialist.   By that time I was already well on - $3\frac{1}{2}$ months.   I just had to accept it.'

In addition some mothers had tried to abort themselves.

'I tried to get rid of it myself.   I took a gallon of castor oil but it didn't work.   I drank gin and took all sorts of stuff to try and get rid of it but nothing worked.   It didn't occur to try and see anybody else about an abortion.'

The proportion of mothers who said they had thought of getting an abortion was 17% of those who said they had not intended to get pregnant.   This proportion, who had considered abortion when they found they were unintentionally pregnant, varied with:

1 The birth order.   It was 14% for first births, fell to 9% for second births, then rose to 23% and 26% for third and fourth births respectively, falling slightly to 19% for higher birth orders.

2 The interval between the last two births.   It was 12% for birth intervals under three years, 25% for intervals between three and five years, 29% for longer intervals.

3 Whether they had been using any method of birth control around the time they became pregnant - 20% for those who were, 13% for those who were not.

4 The length of their marriage.   It was 17% of those married for less than a year, fell to 6% of those married between one and four years, then rose to 18% of those married between four and ten years, and 28% for those married for ten years or more.

5   Whether they hoped for further children.   The proportion was
    13% among those who did or were uncertain, 19% among those who
    did not.
6   Their views on abortion.   It was 23% among those who thought
    that any woman should be able to get an abortion if she wanted
    it, 15% among those who did not think that any woman should be
    able to get one but thought a woman with several children ought
    to be able to get an abortion if she wanted it, and 8% among
    those who did not.
7   Their age.   Older mothers of 30 or more were more likely to
    have thought about it - 26% of them had done so compared with
    14% of younger mothers.

The proportion did not vary to any significant extent with social
class or the mother's religion.   (It was 16% among those who were
Catholics, 16% among those who said they were Church of England, 19%
among those with other religious affiliations, and 20% among those
with none.)

So the ones most likely to have considered abortion for an
unintended pregnancy were those married for ten or more years, older
mothers, and those with an interval of five or more years since
their previous baby.   These characteristics are all interrelated.

When it came to considering abortions in the future, those who
did not want another child were asked whether they might try to get
an abortion if they found they were pregnant.   ('Supposing you found
you were pregnant - how would you feel about it?' 'Do you think you
think you might try to get an abortion?')   Thirteen per cent said
they would, 7% were uncertain, and 80% said they would not.   But
of course their expressed views on this are not necessarily a
reliable indication of future behaviour.   The ways in which the
proportion who said they might try to get an abortion varied with
various characteristics of the mother are shown in Table 49.

The proportion was relatively low, 11%, for those with one or two
children, rose to 26% for those with four, but was only 9% among
those with five or more, suggesting once again that mothers with
large families of that size are in many other ways an unusual group.
The proportion varied in a U-shaped way with the space between the
last two children, was higher among middle-class than among working-
class mothers, increased with the length of marriage, and was
related, to some extent, to their views on abortion.   However, even
among those with liberal views on abortion, who apparently favoured
abortion on request, only one in five of those not wanting another
baby said they would try to get an abortion.   If there is a
correlation between their statements and future action, it would
seem that relatively few would try to get an abortion for a future
unwanted pregnancy.   An even smaller proportion, 2%, said they
were prepared to consider an abortion for spacing purposes.   (This
was based on the mothers who hoped they would have another child.
They were asked how long a time they would like to have between the
last baby and the next one and then, if their preferred time was a
year or more and they were not already pregnant, 'Supposing you
found you were pregnant before that, do you think you might try to
get an abortion?')

TABLE 49   Variations in the proportion of mothers who might try
to get an abortion

	Proportion who might try to get an abortion	Number of mothers not wanting another child (= 100%)
Number of children		
One	11%	62
Two	11%	295
Three	18%	135
Four	26%	38
Five or more	9%	22
Space between last two children		
Less than $1\frac{1}{2}$ years	24%	59
$1\frac{1}{2}$ years < 4 years	10%	292
4 years or longer	18%	119
Social class		
Middle class	19%	154
Working class	12%	373
Length of marriage		
Less than five years	10%	261
5 years or longer	17%	288
Religion		
Catholic	13%	61
Church of England	12%	373
Other protestant	12%	65
Other	28%	32
None	30%	20
Views on abortion		
Liberal	18%	285
Intermediate	13%	99
Restrictive	4%	160
Attitude to future pregnancy		
Very upset	30%	212
Fairly upset	6%	161
Not very upset	1%	172
All mothers not wanting another child	13%	552

It is sometimes argued that the possibility of getting an
abortion discourages the use of effective contraception.   In fact,
amongst those who said they would consider an abortion, the
proportion who were not using relatively reliable methods of
contraception (pill, cap, coil or sheath) was 9%, whereas it was
double that, 19%, among those who said they would not consider an
abortion or were uncertain.

For this sample then, with its built-in bias against women who
have had an abortion, the great majority would apparently accept

an unwanted pregnancy rather than think of getting an abortion.
Contraception is much the preferred method of fertility control.
But although most reject the idea of abortion for themselves almost
half were apparently in favour of abortion on request.   The
proportion who thought abortion should be generally available to a
woman with several children had doubled between 1967/68 and 1973.

Chapter 7

CONTRACEPTIVE SERVICES AND DISCUSSION OF BIRTH CONTROL

It was suggested in the last chapter that one reason why more people were not using relatively reliable methods of contraception might lie in the inadequacy, inappropriateness, or unacceptability of contraceptive services. This possibility is examined in this chapter.

CHANGES OVER TIME

In both the 1967/68 study and the 1973 one mothers were asked if they had talked about methods of birth control with the various people listed in Table 50, and who they had found most helpful. The comparison shows that professional people played a greater role in 1973 than in 1967/68.

By 1973 the general practitioner was not only the most common source of professional help, he was the person most often reported, by 29% of the mothers, as being the most helpful person to whom they had talked. Nevertheless, a third of the mothers said they had never discussed methods of birth control with their doctor.

The proportion of mothers who said they had talked to a doctor at hospital and the proportion who had talked to a health visitor about contraception had both doubled since 1967/68. But even so the proportion who said they had not done so was still three-quarters in both cases.

The only group of people with whom mothers had significantly less discussion in 1973 were friends or neighbours. Presumably this was because more of them had found more satisfactory alternatives. However, two-fifths of the mothers had either found a non-professional or no one at all most helpful.

Among fathers there was less change. The proportions who had talked to a general practitioner about birth control were similar on the two studies, 16% in 1967/68, 15% in 1973. But in the more recent inquiry a higher proportion of the fathers said they had discussed methods of birth control with their wives, 94% compared with 84%. However, when asked who they had found most helpful more of the fathers in 1973 than in 1967/68 said no one. This proportion had also increased among the mothers which suggests a

high level of expectations since the proportion who said they had
not talked to anyone had not changed for mothers and had fallen for
fathers.   These differences are shown in Table 51.

TABLE 50   Discussion about methods of birth control

	Any discussion		Most helpful person	
	1967/68	1973	1967/68	1973
	%	%	%	%
General practitioner	48	65	20	29
Family planning clinic doctor	23	29	12	14
Doctor at hospital	12	25	3	5
Doctor at welfare clinic	3	8	1	1
Private doctor	2	3	1	1
Health visitor	13	26	3	5
Nurse/midwife at hospital	3	10	1	1
Nurse/midwife at clinic or home	5	12	1	2
Vicar, priest		2		-
School teacher	4	1	-	-
Chemist		1		-
Friends or neighbours	77	60	16	9
Husband	90	94	20	13
Mother		32		2
Father	50	6	13	-
Other relatives		38		4
People having baby at same time	40	46	1	1
Other non-professionals	1	2	-	1
No one	4	4	8**	12**
Number of mothers (=100%)	1,491	1,469	1,396*	1,415*

*   Some mothers gave more than one answer and have therefore been excluded.
** These include the mothers who had not talked to anyone and those who said that none of the people they talked to had been helpful.

TABLE 51   The most helpful person with whom mothers and fathers discussed birth control

	Mothers		Fathers	
	1967/68	1973	1967/68	1973
	%	%	%	%
Doctor	37	50	12	13
Other professional	5	8	2	1
Husband or wife	20	13	47	41
Friend, relative or non-professional	30	17	24	17
No one helpful but some discussion	4	8	3	23
No discussion	4	4	12	5
Number of parents (= 100%)	1,396	1,415	242	243

While mothers had become more dependent on professional advice, fathers seemed to be less satisfied with their discussions with non-professionals.

Another change was in the proportion of mothers who felt their doctor had 'enough time to talk about things like family planning'. In 1967/68 this was 46%, in 1973 it had risen slightly to 52%. For fathers the trend was, if anything, in the opposite direction and the proportion who felt their doctor had enough time to discuss family planning had fallen from 40% in 1967/68 to 33% in 1973 - although this difference might have occurred by chance.   These results suggest that while professional help became more available and more acceptable to mothers during those five years, it might still constitute a barrier for some couples.

RELATIONSHIP WITH DOCTORS

When professional help is available it is not always thought to be relevant or helpful.   Of the mothers who had talked to a doctor about birth control, three-fifths said they had found a doctor most helpful but a quarter of them had found discussions with friends and relatives more helpful.   And of those who said no one had been helpful, three-fifths had had some discussion with a doctor.

Mothers who thought their doctor had time to talk about birth control were more likely to have talked to him about it than those who did not, 71% compared with 62%.   Or, looking at this the other way round, the proportion who felt he had time was somewhat higher among those who had talked to their general practitioner than among those who had not, 57% against 42%.

Their comments give some indication of the nature of their relationship.   First from those who had talked about it and thought their doctor had time:

'He's very good.   In fact he has been a great help at calming my anxiety about wanting to continue with my career.   He says it's far better to be honest.'

'He isn't too bad - easy to talk to.   I had it for heavy periods as well as for birth control and it's certainly helped the periods.   He did explain what it did.   We only talked about the pill.'

'But I don't think he knows much about it.   He hasn't personal experience.   He's a bachelor.   He does have time.   He suggested after the little one was born that I went to the family planning clinic or he would prescribe the pill.'

Next from those who thought he would have time, but who had not talked to him about it:

'He really is nice that way - you can talk to him.   I'm sure he would if I wanted to talk about it.'

'Yes, I think so - but I feel they have enough to do and I prefer the family planning clinic doctor.   She's very easy to talk to and helpful.   But yes, I think my doctor would make time if I wanted him to.'

'Well I'm so embarrassed - it's only my fault.   I'm really surprised that I'm talking to you like this.   Yes, I'm certain

he would but I could not ask him.   I just could not.'
Then from those who had talked to him but felt he did not have
enough time:
   'He probably wouldn't have talked last time except it was my
   post-natal.   Normally he wouldn't have time, I don't think.'
   'I wouldn't say she has enough time, but she does spend some
   time on it if you want to.'
   'I don't think he wants to make enough time.   I had to persist
   and question him.'
   'I asked him and he just said if I get it off him I'd have to
   pay, so I might as well go to the clinic - it's free there.'
Finally from some who had not talked to their doctor about it and
did not think he had time for such discussions:
   'They're very busy.   They do a good job but wouldn't have time
   for that sort of thing.'
   'They seem to want to rush you in and get you out as quickly as
   they can.'
   'Whenever I go it's straight in and straight out.   He seems
   very rushed.'
A small group, 6%, of mothers were not prepared to say whether or
not their doctor had time to discuss things or not:
   'I don't know.   I've never really gone to him to talk about
   things like that.   I'm too shy.'
   How much difference does their relationship with their doctor
make to the methods of contraception they were using?   There was
not difference between those who thought their doctor had time to
talk about family planning and those who did not.   But the small
group who did not answer this question directly were less likely to
be taking the pill, 29% compared with 44%.   And they were much less
likely to have talked to a general practitioner about birth control,
29% against 67%.
   It is difficult to assess how much difference discussion with a
doctor makes to the methods of birth control being used because the
more reliable methods depend on a doctor's intervention.   One in
twelve of those who had consulted a doctor were not using any method
of contraception compared with a quarter of those who had not done
so.   A sixth of the former group were using a sheath against almost
half of the latter, and the proportions relying on withdrawal were
one in twenty compared with nearly one in five.   Altogether two-
thirds of the mothers who had talked to a doctor about birth control
were using a medical method, but a third were not.   Who discusses
birth control with whom?

SOCIAL CLASS

In the earlier 1967/68 study mothers with husbands in non-manual
jobs were more likely to have discussed birth control with a general
practitioner and with a family planning clinic doctor, but discussions about birth control with the health visitor were more common
for working-class mothers with husbands in manual jobs.   In 1973
there were no differences between middle- and working-class mothers
in the proportion who had discussed birth control with a general
practitioner or with a health visitor, but there was still a marked

trend in the proportion who had done so with a doctor at a family planning clinic from 41% of those with husbands in professional jobs to 19% of the wives of unskilled workers.   Another difference in 1973 was in the proportion who had talked to a doctor at the hospital which was slightly higher among working-class than middle-class mothers, 27% compared with 21%, and more of the middle- than of the working-class mothers had seen a private doctor about it, 5% against 2%.   The few mothers who said they had not talked to anyone at all about birth control were all working-class.   They made up 5% of working-class mothers, 4% of all mothers.

When it came to the person they had found most helpful, more of the middle- than the working-class said it was a doctor, 57% compared with 48%.   A quarter of the middle-class but a third of the working-class mothers had found a non-professional most helpful. In spite of this there was no difference in the proportions who said they had discussed it with the different types of non-professional people listed in Table 50, except that fewer working-class mothers had discussed it with their husbands, 92% against 98%.

SIZE OF FAMILY

In the earlier study the proportion of mothers who had talked to a hospital doctor rose from 9% of those with one child to 32% of those with five or more.   In the current study the rise is just as dramatic - but at a higher level, starting at 17% and rising to 66% (see Table 52).   In both studies the proportion who had been to a family planning clinic varied little with family size, but the pattern of discussions with the health visitor had changed quite markedly.   In 1967/68 there was a clear trend with family size from 7% of those with one child to 44% of those with seven or more. In the current study 22% of mothers with one child had talked to a health visitor compared with 30% of those with two or three, but more of the mothers with two or three children said they had talked to a health visitor than mothers with larger families of four or more, 22%.   It would seem that in 1973 health visitors were more likely to discuss birth control with mothers of two or three children than in 1967/68 but, if anything, rather less likely in 1973 to talk to mothers with five or more children about it.

Looking at discussions with non-professional people, the group that stands out are the mothers with five or more children.   They were the ones least likely to have talked to friends or neighbours or to their mothers about birth control.   In terms of the most helpful person, the ones with large families of five or more were the least likely to say a non-professional person was most helpful. There are a number of possible explanations for this.   One is that people who, for one reason or another, have little close contact with relatives and friends may deliberately compensate for this by having a large family.   Another possibility is that it is the informal network of family and friends which is important in supporting couples with the establishment and maintenance of effective contraception, and therefore those with little contact with family and friends, lacking this help, tend to have more children. Certainly mothers who had not talked about birth control with

relatives, friends or other non-professionals were more likely to be
having unprotected intercourse, 29% compared with 10% of other
mothers.   They were less likely to be using the relatively reliable
methods - pill, cap, IUD, sheath, or sterilization - 55% against 81%,
but no less likely to use the other less reliable methods, 16%
compared with 9%.   They were also much less likely to have discussed
it with a doctor, 44% against 85%.

TABLE 52   Family size and discussion of birth control

	Mothers' number of children				
	One	Two	Three	Four	Five or more
Discussed methods of birth control with:	%	%	%	%	%
General practitioner	57	70	67	78	70
Family planning clinic doctor	29	29	32	30	23
Doctor at hospital	17	25	33	44	66
Doctor at welfare clinic	6	8	12	8	11
Private doctor	3	4	2	4	4
Health visitor	22	31	29	22	23
Nurse/midwife at hospital	9	10	11	16	15
Nurse/midwife at clinic/home	8	12	16	16	25
Vicar, priest	1	2	1	3	-
School teacher	2	1	-	1	-
Other professional	1	-	-	-	-
Friends or neighbours	57	64	65	58	42
Husband	94	95	93	91	85
Mother	36	31	27	32	15
Father	6	7	4	6	6
Other relatives	36	43	40	35	28
People having baby at same time	46	49	45	44	36
Other non-professionals	2	2	1	1	2
No one	4	3	3	4	9
No.of mothers (=100%)	609	502	222	77	53
Most helpful person:	%	%	%	%	%
A doctor	45	55	52	52	56
Other professional	7	8	8	8	12
Non-professional	35	27	28	32	16
No one	13	10	12	8	16
No.of mothers (=100%)	574	490	214	72	51

MOTHERS' AGE

Mothers in their late twenties were the ones most likely to have
talked to a family planning clinic doctor about birth control.
The proportions were 28% of those under 25, 35% of those aged
25-29, and 22% of older mothers. Older mothers of 30 or more
were also rather less likely to have discussed it with a health
visitor, 21% compared with 28% of younger mothers. But older
mothers were more likely to have talked to a hospital doctor. The
proportions who had done so rose from 19% of those under 25, to
29% of those aged 25-29, and 35% of those aged 30 or more.
   However, the main differences with age lay in the proportions
discussing birth control with their parents. This can be seen
in Table 53.

TABLE 53 Age and discussion of birth control with non-professionals

	Mothers' age				
	Under 20	20-24	25-29	30-34	35 or more
Discussed methods of birth control with:	%	%	%	%	%
Friends and neighbours	54	63	65	58	36
Husband	97	94	96	90	87
Mother	53	34	32	21	7
Father	8	6	6	6	1
Other relatives	43	39	41	31	27
People having baby at same time	52	48	51	43	20
Other non-professionals	2	2	2	2	1
None of these	3	3	2	7	9
No. of mothers (=100%)	145	543	484	200	86

   The gradient in the proportion discussing birth control with
their mothers is steep, dropping from 53% of those under 20 to 7%
of those aged 35 or more. This could be a generation difference
but memory may also contribute. However, the fact that the
proportion who had never discussed it with their husbands rose from
3% of those under 20 to 13% of those aged 35 or more suggests that
there is a definite generation effect. Older mothers, of 30 or
more, were also less likely to have talked to friends and neighbours,
other relatives, and people having a baby at the same time.

METHODS DISCUSSED

Mothers were more likely to have discussed the pill with doctors
than any other methods. Nine out of ten of the mothers who had
talked to a doctor about any method of birth control said the pill
had been mentioned, compared with two-fifths who had talked about
the IUD, the method next most frequently discussed with doctors.

General practitioners in particular seemed likely to limit their
discussion to the pill: comparing mothers who had talked to a
general practitioner with mothers who had talked to other doctors,
the proportions who had discussed the pill were 90% and 83%, but
the cap 24% and 40%, IUD 35% and 51%, sheath 17% and 25%, and
withdrawal 3% and 7%.   This ties up with results from other
studies which have shown that some general practitioners tend to
equate family planning with the pill and to advise that method
almost exclusively (Cartwright and Waite, 1972).
     When mothers were asked whether they would like to know more
about different methods of contraception, the pill was the method
most often mentioned, but nearly as many mothers wanted more
information about male sterilization. The IUD and female sterilization came next (see Table 54). Over half did not want to know
more about any methods.

TABLE 54   Proportion of mothers who would like to know more about
different methods of contraception

Would like to know more about:	%
Female sterilization	13
Male sterilization	18
Pill	20
Cap	7
IUD	15
Sheath	4
Withdrawal	4
Safe period	7
Chemicals	5
None	56
Number of mothers, excluding those using sterilization (= 100%)	1,339

     Rather more of the working- than of the middle-class mothers
would have liked more information about some methods, 46% compared
with 39%. There was little variation in this proportion with
mothers' age except that few, 25%, of those aged 35 or more would
have liked to know more.   Desire for additional information about
the pill declined from 26% of those under 20 to 15% of those aged
30-34 and 12% of those aged 35 or more, but the proportion who
would have liked to know more about male sterilization increased
from 9% of those under 20 to 24% of those aged 30-34 then fell to
5% for older mothers.
     Mothers currently using the sheath, withdrawal, or nothing at
all were more likely to say they would like to know more about
contraception than those taking the pill or using the cap or coil -
50% against 39%.   Those who had talked to a doctor about birth
control were no more or less likely to want to know more about some

methods than mothers who had not done so.   But mothers who had
discussed it with a doctor were less likely than the others to want
to know more about the pill, 19% compared with 27%, or cap, 6%
against 11%, but there was no significant difference in relation to
the IUD or sterilization.   This illustrates again the emphasis
placed on the pill by the general practitioner, the doctor most
frequently consulted.

ADVICE AND HELP ABOUT THE PILL

Three-quarters of the mothers who had ever taken the pill had
first obtained the prescription from their general practitioner,
most of the others from a family planning clinic.   And whereas
92% of those first getting it from a general practitioner had
continued to do so this compares with 71% of those first getting
it from a family planning clinic, the other 29% had later changed
and obtained prescriptions elsewhere, mostly from a general
practitioner.   Those who had changed were asked why they had done
so.   The main reason for preferring to get a prescription from
their general practitioner was that it was more convenient, but
one in ten of those changing from the family planning clinic to
their own doctor had done so for more personal reasons:
    'Down at the clinic you're just one of many.   It's public too.'
    'I told the doctor I was on the pill and he said "Why don't you
    come to me for it?"   I didn't like to because we weren't
    married, but he said that's silly, it's better than an abortion.'
Three-tenths of those who had switched and later got their pills
from a family planning clinic did so because it was cheaper or
free, a quarter because they found the clinic took more time or
gave them a more thorough examination.
    'Mainly because I was going to be on the pill a fair length
    of time and I felt they might have more time and that I ought
    to be examined internally.   My G.P. never examined me internally.
    I do think the family planning clinic gives you more time for
    discussion and they are more interested.   Another thing, I
    wanted to get used to intimate examinations before I had the
    baby.   The family planning clinic made it easier - amongst
    other women.'
    'Never even had a check up from him (G.P.) and I wanted to be
    safe.   He just gave me a prescription and never asked me any-
    thing.'
One in ten found their general practitioner reluctant or unwilling.
    'I had to.   The doctor would only give me one month's supply
    as he's a Catholic.'
On the earlier study, 'Parents and Family Planning Services',
it was found that mothers who got their pills from a family planning
clinic were more likely to be examined than those who got them
from their general practitioner, and mothers who were examined were
more likely to continue to take the pill and less likely to report
symptoms which they felt were associated with it.   In the current
study there was no difference between mothers getting their pills
from a clinic or a general practitioner in the proportion still
taking it or in the proportion reporting associated symptoms.

The 324 mothers who had stopped taking the pill were asked whether anyone had advised them to do this; 71% of them said no and most of these had stopped because they wanted to become pregnant, although a third had done so because of anxiety or experience of side effects.

Of the ones who had been advised to stop taking the pill over half, 56%, had been given this advice by their general practitioner, 11% by a clinic doctor, 15% by some other professional and 19% by their husbands. Since the ratio of mothers who had ever got their pills from a general practitioner as opposed to a family planning clinic was 3:1 while the ratio of mothers who had been advised to give it up by a general practitioner rather than a clinic doctor was 5:1, this suggests that general practitioners gave this advice rather more readily than doctors at family planning clinics.

ADVICE AND HELP ABOUT STERILIZATION

Fourteen per cent of the mothers had discussed the possibility of sterilization with someone during their last pregnancy or since the survey baby had been born but neither they nor their husbands had been sterilized. A further 10% said they would have liked to discuss it, and as shown earlier 4% had been sterilized themselves and the husbands of a further 3%. So sterilization had not been discussed with about a third of the mothers who were interested.

Among those who had talked to a professional about the possibility of sterilization, 45% had discussed it with a hospital doctor, 47% with a general practitioner, and 18% with another professional. Half had talked about female sterilization only, a fifth about male sterilization, and three-tenths about both. Hospital doctors were more likely than general practitioners to discuss female sterilization only, 67% against 40%. while general practitioners more often discussed male sterilization only, 31% against 2%; three-tenths of both discussed both possibilities. Slightly less than half the discussions, 44%, were initiated by the mother, rather more, 56%, by the professional. When the mother raised it the discussion was less often restricted just to female sterilization, 39% compared with 57% when the professional raised it, and more often covered male sterilization, 61% against 43%.

SOME SUGGESTIONS

It can be argued that birth control services are relatively unimportant from a demographic point of view. People certainly managed to restrict their fertility before modern methods of birth control were invented. But once such methods are available people may become less willing to use older, more traditional, methods, and certainly use of the sheath, withdrawal, and safe period declined between 1967/68 and 1973. However, the proportion of unintended pregnancies is still high, so that theoretically an improvement in the acceptability of contraceptive services might lead to further reductions in the birth rate. The greatest potential for reducing unwanted pregnancies is among the young - both married and unmarried.

For them, the most obvious way to make effective contraception more readily accessible would be to make the pill available without prescription.   For younger women the pill appears to be a generally acceptable form of birth control.   And for the unmarrieds, and especially the sexually inexperienced, the present process of obtaining the pill is probably often a formidable barrier.   It may, theoretically, be desirable for some groups of people at any rate to have some medical supervision when taking the pill.   But it seems dubious whether much of the supervision given at the moment justifies the barrier the process creates.   As the 'Lancet' pointed out, 'if one bears in mind that adverse effects can seldom be predicted from routine physical examination the case for taking the pill off prescription and letting it go on general sale seems strong' ('Lancet', 1974).

One irony of the present situation is that the pill, IUD, male and·female sterilization all depend on medical intervention yet much of the advice and help from doctors tends to be directed to a single method of contraception.   But the acceptability of the methods varies for different people.   There is much anxiety about the health hazards of the pill among older mothers and many women who are quite prepared to take it at certain stages are reluctant to do so for the larger part of their fertile life.   For many mothers who have the children they want and who have reached the stage when they would be unwilling to start childbearing again, sterilization would seem to be an acceptable method.   But if the medical profession is reluctant to sterilize women unless they already have three children, the majority of women who only want two children will not be able to use this method.   The views of mothers about different methods of contraception suggest that the IUD would be acceptable for many, particularly those who have had all the children they want at the moment but who may still want to keep their options open for a while.   Yet it is often not easy to get such an appliance fitted.

The needs of younger women are now well recognized although appropriate services and methods may not exist at the moment.   The needs of older women seem less well recognized, most seem prepared to use existing methods but the services appear less sensitive to their needs.   In theory a wider choice of reliable methods is available to them;   in practice it does not seem to be so.

Chapter 8

SUB-FERTILITY

Mothers who said they wanted further children were asked whether
they thought they would be able to manage to have exactly the
number they decided on or whether they thought they might have
more or fewer children.   Three-quarters said they thought they
would have the exact number, 7% that they might have fewer, 9%
that they might have more and the rest were uncertain.   So, for
those with incomplete families, sub-fertility was considered a
possibility by marginally fewer than those who felt over-production
was more likely.   Those who did not want more children were asked
how they would feel if they found they were pregnant and if they
thought this was 'quite likely to happen' (10% thought so), 'rather
unlikely to happen' (33%), or 'very unlikely to happen' (57%).
It has been shown earlier that 26% of those who did not want more
had already had more children than they intended, and in this
sample 'too many' is a more likely possibility than 'too few'.
This chapter is concerned with the less common problem.

EXTENT OF SUB-FERTILITY

No infertile couples are included in this study, the information
here relates only to the possible extent of sub-fertility among
couples who have had at least one baby.   Three per cent of the
mothers said they had had difficulty conceiving in the past, 4%
had had difficulty in carrying a baby to term, less than 1% had
been sterilized for reasons other than birth control, and 3% said
there were other reasons why they and their husbands might have
difficulty in having more children if they wanted to.   ('Have you
any reason to think that you and your husband could not have more
children if you wanted to - that you might have any difficulty
becoming pregnant again - or difficulty going on with the pregnancy
until the baby was born?')   A fifth of this last small group were
no longer living together.   Most of the others made comments which
suggested that they felt they should not have further children
rather than that they were unlikely to conceive.   A fifth had had
a Caesarian last time.   Other comments were:
   'I'd like more children but I've got kidney trouble and the
   doctor advised me not to.'

'I'm rhesus negative and he's rhesus positive.   It may make a
difference with the second child.   It might be a blue baby.'
'I've had sickness right the way through, especially with the
first, and I was depressed carrying Matthew.'
'Just a premonition - no real logical reason.   I felt this
feeling all the time I was carrying Amanda - and I was proved
wrong.'
One problem in evaluating mothers' statements that they had
experienced difficulty in conceiving is that there is no information
about people's expectations about how long it is likely to take them
to conceive.   Two-thirds of those who said they had had difficulty
.onceiving in the past had been having unprotected intercourse for
two years or longer before they became pregnant with the survey
baby ('Round about the time you became pregnant - that time - were
you and your husband using any method of birth control?' IF NO,
'For how long had you been having intercourse without taking
precautions - up until you became pregnant?') - and another fifth,
22%, had taken between one and two years.   So nine out of ten of
them had taken a year or more to conceive compared with a fifth of
other mothers.   The distribution for all mothers is shown in
Table 55.

TABLE 55   Time taken to become pregnant

Length of time had been having inter-course without taking precautions before they became pregnant with survey baby:	All mothers	Mothers not taking precautions	Mothers not taking precautions who intended to become pregnant
	%	%	%
Not at all - taking precautions when became pregnant	22	-	-
Less than 3 months	37	48	50
3 months < 6 months	14	18	18
6 months < 1 year	10	13	13
1 year < 2 years	7	9	8
2 years or longer	10	12	11
No. of mothers (= 100%)	1,452	1,135	909

The 19% of mothers intending to become pregnant who took a year
or more to conceive may be compared with 13% of women on another
study who had not become pregnant a year after stopping taking the
pill in order to do so. (The Royal College of General Practitioners,
1974, p.97. These data were said to overestimate the proportion of
women who had failed to conceive though wishing to do so, p.75.)
A possible reason for the greater length of time taken in this study
may be age differences in the two groups. (Age differences in the
Royal College of General Practitioners' study are not yet available.)

The suggestion that the use of the pill has the effect of making a woman conceive more rapidly after she discontinues it has not been borne out by data (Ryder and Westoff, 1971, p.184).

Earlier it was shown that 19% of those who had two or more children would have preferred to have the last two children closer together and 10% of mothers would have liked to have the survey baby earlier than they did.   But some may have made these judgments retrospectively - they did not necessarily try to have the baby earlier, they just wished afterwards that they had done so.   In fact, 36% of mothers who said at the interview that they would have liked their survey baby earlier had had unprotected intercourse for two or more years and another 15% for between one and two years. So, as suggested in Chapter 2, possibly half the mothers had taken longer than they wanted to become pregnant, the other half who said they would have preferred the birth to be earlier may have been expressing a retrospective assessment of the timing.

To sum up, the various indicators of sub-fertility on this study suggest that while as many as a fifth may have experienced delays in conceiving, the proportion of mothers who expect difficulties in achieving their desired family size because of sub-fertility is smaller;   4% of those who wanted another child thought they might have difficulty in conceiving, 4% in carrying a baby to term, and 2% might deliberately restrict the number of children they have for health reasons or because of difficulties in childbearing.

In trying to identify the sorts of women who are sub-fertile the main index that has been taken is the length of time taken to become pregnant with the survey baby for those not using any method of birth control around the time of conception.

AGE AND LENGTH OF MARRIAGE

The length of time it took to become pregnant was clearly related to the mother's age.   This is shown in Table 56.

TABLE 56   Age and length of time having unprotected intercourse before coming pregnant

Length of time having unprotected intercourse:	Age of mother				
	Under 20	20-24	25-29	30-34	35 or more
	%	%	%	%	%
Less than 3 months	46	52	51	34	29
3 months < 6 months	21	21	18	14	11
6 months < 1 year	18	13	11	14	11
1 year < 2 years	12	9	8	9	2
2 years or longer	3	5	12	29	47
Number of mothers (= 100%)*	113	438	381	141	55

* Excluding those who became pregnant while they were using some method of birth control.

Those who became pregnant while they were using precautions have been excluded from this table.   The proportion of them was a fifth of those under 20 and a third of those aged 30 or more.   If they are included the proportion who took two years or longer to conceive rose from 2% of those under 20 to 30% of those aged 35 or more.

A somewhat similar trend was found with length of marriage.   The proportion having unprotected intercourse for two years or more before they became pregnant rose from 3% of those married less than a year to 58% of those married for 15 years or more.   Age and length of marriage are of course closely related.   But both appear to have some effect on the time taken to become pregnant.   This is illustrated by the data in Table 57 which is confined to mothers aged 20 and over who had been married for less than 10 years. Similar findings were reported from the USA (Freedman et al., 1959, pp.40-1).

TABLE 57 Age, length of marriage and proportion having intercourse for two years or more before they became pregnant

Proportion taking two years or more before becoming pregnant		
	Mothers' age	
20-24	25-29	30 or more
Length of marriage		
Less than 3 years 4% (273)	6% (85)	13% (31)
3 years < 5 years 5% (123)	8% (118)	29% (21)
5 years < 10 years 12% (42)	16% (166)	26% (62)

Figures in brackets are the number of mothers on which the percentages are based (= 100%).   Those who became pregnant while taking precautions have been excluded.

FREQUENCY OF INTERCOURSE

A possible explanation for the trends of both age and length of marriage with the time taken to conceive might be variations in the frequency of intercourse. ('Have you and your husband had intercourse in the last seven days?' IF YES, 'How many times?') Certainly the reported frequency of intercourse was clearly related to mother's age and to length of marriage.   The relationship with age is shown in Table 58.

The only other published data on frequency of intercourse in this country come from Gorer (1971, pp.114-15).   He asked: 'About how often do you have intercourse?' He divided his sample of married people into three groups - those with what he described as a high rate of three times a week or more, 24% of his sample compared with 29% in this study;   those with a medium rate of more than once a week but less than three, 36% of his sample 25% of this one; and those with a low rate of once a week or less, 37% compared with 46%. Differences in the age distribution of the two samples would lead one to expect a lower frequency in Gorer's study since the proportion aged 35 or more was 41% in his sample (which was confined to people aged 45 or less) compared with 6% on this study.   But his question seems likely to lead to a higher estimate.   In the present study 3% said they had had intercourse more frequently than usual in the weeks asked about, 28% said they had had it less frequently.   The most likely explanation for this disparity would seem to be that people perceive themselves as having intercourse more frequently than they do in fact.

TABLE 58   Age and reported frequency of intercourse

	Mothers' age					All mothers
	Under 20	20-24	25-29	30-34	35 or more	
	%	%	%	%	%	%
Not in week before interview or in the week before that	7 ⎤	6 ⎤	9 ⎤	11 ⎤	22 ⎤	9 ⎤
Not in week before interview but in the week before that	10 ⎦ ⎰17	13 ⎦ ⎰19	14 ⎦ ⎰23	25 ⎦ ⎰36	15 ⎦ ⎰37	15 ⎦ ⎰24
Once in week	15	20	24	24	29	22
Twice in week	28	25	29	24	15	25
Three times before	18	19	15	10	10	16
Four times inter-	4	9	6	4	5	7
Five times view	8	4	2	⎤	⎤	3
Six times	3	2	–	⎰2	⎰4	1
Seven or more	7	2	1	⎦	⎦	2
Average number	2.47	2.10	1.72	1.33	1.37	1.86
No. of mothers* (= 100%)	133	521	457	186	78	1,379

* Six per cent of mothers were not prepared to answer the question about intercourse. This did not vary significantly with age.

In the current study the average reported frequency of intercourse fell from 2.58 for those married less than a year to 1.24 for those married 15 years or more.   The relationship between age, length of marriage and frequency of intercourse is shown in Table 59 for mothers aged 20 or more who had been married less than ten years.

These data suggest that age has more effect than length of marriage on frequency of intercourse.

Coming back to the question of sub-fertility, Table 60 shows that the proportion who took two or more years to become pregnant fell from 17% of those who did not have intercourse at all in the week before interview to 8% of those who had it four or more times. But apart from this the relationship is not striking.

TABLE 59   Age, length of marriage and frequency of intercourse

Average reported frequency of intercourse in week before interview

	Mothers' age		
	20-24	25-29	30 or more
Length of marriage:			
Less than 3 years	2.10 (325)	1.69 (95)	1.59 (34)
3 years < 5 years	2.24 (137)	1.76 (136)	1.17 (23)
5 years < 10 years	1.73 (59)	1.77 (209)	1.30 (82)

TABLE 60   Frequency of intercourse and time taken to become pregnant

	Number of times had intercourse in week before interview					
Time taken to become pregnant:	0	1	2	3	4 or more	Not answered
	%	%	%	%	%	%
Less than 3 months	42	45	54	50	49	43
3 months < 6 months	17	22	18	16	19	17
6 months < 1 year	15	11	13	13	14	9
1 year < 2 years	9	9	5	11	10	14
2 years or longer	17	13	10	10	8	17
Number of mothers	249	228	273	170	144	66

When the relationship of age and frequency of intercourse on the time taken to conceive is considered (see Table 61), it appears that the effect of age remains but within age groups the frequency of intercourse in the week before interview did not seem to be related to the proportion who had taken two years or more to become pregnant.

TABLE 61   Age, frequency of intercourse and the proportion taking two or more years to conceive

Proportion taking two or more years to conceive

Number of times had intercourse in week before interview:	Mothers' age		
	20-24	25-29	30 or more
0	7% (75)	17% (84)	31% (67)
1	2% (88)	12% (83)	40% (43)
2	4% (98)	10% (105)	32% (41)
3	9% (79)	9% (55)	} 26% (27)
4 or more	5% (80)	15% (33)	

One difficulty in interpreting these data on frequency of intercourse is that it is not possible to assess their accuracy (but see James, 1971).   Another problem is that there is no information about the way in which frequency of intercourse over one short period relates to frequency of intercourse at another period in time - over a year earlier when the baby was conceived.   When mothers who said they had intercourse in the week before interview were asked whether the number of times they reported was more often than usual, less often than usual, or about average, the proportion describing it as average increased from 59% of those having it once to 94% of those having it five or more times, and the proportion saying it was less often than usual fell from 39% to none.   Those who did not have intercourse at all were asked if they had had it in the week before that, and if so how many times.   Sixty-three per cent of them said they had, and they averaged 1.98 times in that week compared with an average of 2.43 among those having intercourse in the week before interview.

SOCIAL CLASS

There was some evidence that middle-class mothers became pregnant rather more quickly than working-class mothers, 58% of the former conceived within three months compared with 42% of working-class mothers, but there was no difference between them in the proportion who took two years or longer.   One possible explanation for this was that middle-class people were better informed about the stage in a woman's monthly cycle when she was most likely to become pregnant.   The proportion who knew it was in the middle fell from 78% of mothers with husbands in professional jobs to 32% of mothers married to unskilled workers.   But knowledge of this appeared to be unrelated to the time taken to conceive (this remained true if the analysis was confined to mothers who said they had intended to become pregnant), and the class difference in this remains unexplained.   There was no significant difference between middle- and working-class mothers in the average number of times they reported having intercourse in the seven days before interview.

SIZE OF FAMILY

The proportion having unprotected intercourse for two or more years before they became pregnant increased from 11% of mothers having their first baby to 29% of those having their fifth or later one (see Table 62).
    On the other hand the proportion who said they might have difficulty having further children because they had experienced difficulty conceiving in the past decreased with increasing family size.   It was 4% of those with one child, none of those with four or more.

TABLE 62   Size of family and time taken to conceive

Time taken to conceive:	Number of children				
	One	Two	Three	Four	Five or more
	%	%	%	%	%
Less than 3 months	46	50	48	39	39
3 months < 6 months	20	19	16	17	6
6 months < 1 year	14	11	11	15	16
1 year < 2 years	9	9	9	10	10
2 years or longer	11	11	16	19	29
No. of mothers (=100%)	519	411	128	41	31

The relationship in Table 62 between number of children and the time taken to conceive arose apparently because of the association between age and family size.   Among mothers aged 20-24 and 25-29 the proportion who took two years or more to become pregnant did not vary significantly with family size, but among those aged 30 or more the proportion taking two years or more to conceive was higher, 52%, among those having their first child than among those having their second or third, 28%.   The association with age remained when family size was held constant.

SUMMARY

One in ten of the mothers had experienced a delay of two years or more in becoming pregnant with the survey baby.   This proportion rose with both increasing age and increasing length of marriage, independently.   It was also related to frequency of intercourse, but this effect apparently disappeared when age was held constant. Just over half the mothers having their first baby when they were 30 or more had unprotected intercourse for two or more years before they conceived.   Among those who hoped for further children 4% thought they might have some difficulty conceiving, 4% in carrying the baby to term and 2% mentioned other problems related to health or child-bearing.

CONCOMITANTS OF INTENTIONS

Chapter 9

MOTHERS' PERCEPTIONS OF REASONS FOR FAMILY SIZE

'If you want to know why people do what they do, why not first ask
them?'   This is Hawthorn's adaptation of Allport and he goes on to
warn that 'since human fertility is not entirely determined by
social factors of which the actors are aware, this will of course
not provide all the answers' (Hawthorn, 1970, p.67).   But it would
appear to be a sensible starting point in the search for the
elusive demographer's stone which will explain why people have the
number of children they do.
   This short chapter looks first at the reasons that mothers gave
for not wanting more children.

REASONS FOR NOT WANTING FURTHER CHILDREN

Mothers who hoped they would not have any more children were asked
if they could tell us why they felt like that.   Replies are shown
in Table 63 for mothers with different numbers of children.   The
most common reason, given by half the mothers, was financial.
   'Well they are too expensive for a kick off. I think it's far
   better to have one and do right for it than have a few and scrimp
   and save all the time.'
   'It's bringing them up - the cost of everything.'
Mothers with two children were more likely to give this reason than
those with more or than those with only one. (Peel and Carr, 1975,
also found that people wanting a family of two more often gave
economic reasons for their choice than those wanting three children,
p.45.)
   'Two's enough - for financial reasons.   If I had any more I
   wouldn't be able to keep them.'
   It may be that some of these mothers were giving what they saw
as an acceptable answer to both questions on family size intentions
and their reasons for their choice.   But it could also be that it
is more difficult for mothers to explain why they want the most
usual and acceptable family size.   It may not seem to call for an
explanation and when asked for one mothers may be inclined to give
an obvious or conventional response.   The proportion who gave
finance as a reason for not wanting more children decreased with

increasing age from 61% of those under 25 to 26% of those aged 35
or more.   But when family size was held constant this age difference only persisted among those with two children, from 69% of
those under 25 to 56% of older mothers.   So it is the younger
mothers with two children who are perhaps most likely to feel that
there is a conflict between further children and material goods -
or to give the most immediate and acceptable response to these
sorts of questions.

TABLE 63   Present family size and reasons for not wanting further
children

	Present family size*					All mothers not wanting further children
	One	Two	Three	Four	Five or more	
	%	%	%	%	%	%
Cost, expense, enough to feed, clothe, etc.	41	60	47	45	34	51
Children a problem, hard work, restrict freedom	19	31	28	29	34	28
Fear or dislike of pregnancy/ childbirth. Health problems	38	15	20	15	18	19
Housing	4	6	7	6	3	6
Population, inc. social problems of overcrowding	3	6	4	2	-	4
Own or husband's age	12	9	10	8	5	9
Happy with sex of present children	9	15	9	6	-	11
Like the number already have or got enough or too many	15	25	34	36	55	29
Wants to work	3	3	1	-	-	2
Other reasons	6	2	2	5	3	3
No. of mothers (= 100%)	78	306	169	66	38	660

* Number of children of present marriage.

The next most frequent reason was the problem of looking after children and the restrictions this imposed.

'Three's enough.   Want to have life of our own.   Got to be able to go out and enjoy ourselves.'

'I couldn't cope with any more - especially with the last two so close together.'

Fear or dislike of pregnancy or childbirth or other health problems was mentioned by a fifth of the mothers as a reason for not wanting more, and by two-fifths of those who intended to stick at one child.

'I couldn't go through with it again myself.   I found the first three months very difficult - the mental strain.'

Housing, population problems, wanting to get back to work, and their own or their husband's age were each mentioned by less than one in ten of the mothers, although age was mentioned by two-fifths of the mothers aged 35 or more.

Several mothers gave more than one reason.

'Partly because of the population, and I'm too old and we haven't the room or the money.'

'We've got one of each and we're very happy.   Two is enough to bring up.   I haven't had so much patience this time.'

'It's threefold.   Financial, we don't have any relatives around so no help, both children have problems, and I want to get back to work.'

Mothers who subsequently said they might change their minds about not having further children were less likely to give their own or their spouse's age as a reason, 6% against 11%.   They were also less likely to say they were happy with the number they had already, or had enough or too many, 21% compared with 33%.

REASONS FOR WANTING A PARTICULAR NUMBER OF CHILDREN

Mothers who wanted further children were asked how many children they would like to have altogether, then why they felt like that, and the sort of thing that might make them decide to have more or fewer children. ('Can you say about how many children you would like to have altogether?'   IF ANY DOUBT (a) 'Can you say what is the smallest number of children you would like to have altogether?' (b) 'And what is the largest number?'   'Do you think you might ever chance your mind?'   IF POSSIBLY OR RANGE GIVEN AT PREVIOUS QUESTION (a) 'What sort of thing might make you decide to have more?' (b)'And what sort of thing might make you decide to have fewer?')   Financial reasons again figured in the answers of about half, 53%, of the mothers.

'If we could afford four we would but two seems a more likely number.'

'We can't afford any more than two.   If we became better off for some reason we might make it three, but I think just two.'

Nearly a third, 31%, mentioned a dislike of only children, and this proportion was 42% of those who had one child but wanted more.

'I don't really believe in having only one.   It's not good for them - they don't grow up to know a real family life.   My husband's an only child and he doesn't know what it's all about.'

'Well I've seen an only child and they are either very lonely or
spoilt, especially here in the country with no one to play with.'
Three out of ten wanted a particular sex or sex mix.   This proportion was relatively low, 22%, among those who said they wanted two
children altogether, but was 49% among those who said they wanted
two or three.

'I'd like to have a girl. Would probably have stuck at two if
we'd had a girl.'

'Two completes a family and evens it all out - no one gets left
out or spoilt.   If I had another boy then I might try for a
girl - but not after three boys.   I'd be more than content to
stick at two if the next one turns out to be a girl.'

One in five, but three-fifths of those wanting four or more, said
they liked children, or big families.

'I like big families.   Everyone seems to have two.   It's so
conventional.   There is a problem of money but big families are
very nice and close together.   If money is short we may have
to stop at two but I hope we have three at least.'

'I just like family life, especially if they are as good as
Sandra.   I just love children.'

The difficulties of coping with children (19%) and fear or dislike
of pregnancy or childbirth (10%) were mentioned less often by those
wanting further children than by those who did not.   But housing
was mentioned more often, by 10%, compared with 6%.

'We would like one of each.   If I had a house I might have more
but if we stayed here I wouldn't have any more, there is not
enough room.'

To sum up, for half the mothers economic considerations were
seen as a reason either for not wanting more children or for
limiting the number they wanted.   Finance assumed the greatest
importance among mothers who had or wanted just two children.   The
other main reason for wanting two children only was a dislike of a
single-child family.   Fear or dislike of pregnancy or childbirth
was a frequent reason given for deciding to stick at one child,
wanting a particular sex or sex mix for having three, and liking
children for having four or more.   Housing conditions and wanting
to get back to work were only seldom given as reasons for limiting
family size.

THE BEST NUMBER OF CHILDREN

Woolf found that 'women considered the ideal size of family for
people like themselves (a mean of 2.5 children) was...considerably
lower than the ideal for couples with "no particular worries about
money or anything like that" (3.4 children)' (Woolf, 1971, p.33).
So in her study anxieties about money influenced the number of
children people felt were ideal for them.   In this study mothers
were asked: 'Thinking about couples more or less like yourselves,
what do you think is the best number of children - if any - for
them to have nowadays?'   Eight per cent were not prepared to answer
this.   They felt it was 'up to the couples to decide'.   The
replies of the others are shown in Table 64 where they are compared

with the number of children people already had if they did not want
any more, and the number they said they wanted altogether if they
did want more.

TABLE 64 Best number of children, number hoped for, and present
family size

	Best number of children for 'couples more or less like you'	Present family size of mothers not wanting more	Number wanted by those hoping for more or uncertain
	%	%	%
One	1	12	1
One or two	2	-	-
Two	66	46	50
Two or three	15	-	10
Three	9	26	23
Three or four	2	-	2
Four	4	10	12
Five or more	1	6	2
Average	2.27	2.51	2.61
No.of mothers (= 100%)	1,329	674	769

   Two-thirds thought the best number of children was two, only 3%
felt it might be less, four mothers, less than 1%, said none.   The
average for the 'best' was smaller than that already obtained by
mothers who did not want more children in spite of the 12% who just
had one.   But, as shown earlier, 26% of those not wanting more had
already had more than they intended.
   Expenses again figured prominently in the reasons given for
selecting the best number.   It was mentioned by two-thirds.   But
whereas less than one in twenty gave population pressures as a
reason for not wanting further children themselves, one in five
mentioned this as a reason for thinking that two was the best
number.
   'The population is enough already.   If everyone had five or six
   it would be completely out of control.'
   What was the relationship between their own family size preferences and their views on the best number of children for couples
more or less like themselves?   Among those who wanted further
children a quarter of those who thought the best number of children
was two wanted more than that themselves, while almost a third of
those who thought it was three only wanted two.   Overall, 76%
wanted the number they thought was best, 6% wanted fewer children,
18% more.   Among those who did not want further children 57% had
the number they thought best, 13% had fewer and 30% more.   (Those
who wanted further children thought the best number of children was
slightly higher on average than those who did not want more, 2.35

compared with 2.22.)   So there was a tendency for mothers both to have and to want more than the number they felt was best.   Their comments suggest that the main reasons for this were thinking a smaller number was best because of population pressures, but wanting a larger number to get a particular sex or sex distribution, or because they liked a large family.

Chapter 10

SOCIAL CLASS AND EDUCATION

To cite Hawthorn again, social class data on differential fertility
can only specify the questions that need to be asked, they cannot
answer explanatory questions (Hawthorn, 1970, p.84). At this
stage of trying to identify the relevant questions it seems
appropriate to look at social class and the ways in which it is
related to fertility and some of the intervening variables.

FAMILY SIZE AND SOCIAL CLASS

Table 65 shows the ways in which the different measures of family
size varied with the social class of the baby's father's occupation.

TABLE 65 Social class and family size

| Average number of children: | Social class of baby's father's occupation | | | | | | | All mothers |
	I	II	III N	III M	IV	V	Unclas- sified	
At time of interview	1.96	1.82	1.77	1.92	2.21	2.10	1.88	1.96
At time of interview by those not wanting more	2.57	2.35	2.30	2.54	2.70	2.67	2.42	2.53
Wanted altogether by those wanting more or uncertain	2.89	2.56	2.53	2.57	2.72	2.78	2.63	2.63
Intended*	2.74	2.47	2.43	2.56	2.71	2.72	2.53	2.58
No. of mothers on which averages based								
Not wanting more	42	80	57	280	133	54	31	677
Wanting more or uncertain	48	113	73	327	113	60	35	769
Total	93	201	131	615	250	116	67	1,473

* The intended number of children is the present number of children
for those who do not want further children and the number wanted
altogether by those who do or were uncertain.

101

All the measures were, to some extent, U or J shaped. The mothers whose husbands were in skilled non-manual occupations, such as clerks, cashiers, office machine operators, and commercial travellers were the ones who had and who wanted fewest children. Among those with husbands in manual jobs, those in skilled occupations had and wanted smaller families than those in less skilled jobs. While among the non-manual jobs it was the wives of professional men who wanted the largest families. This U or J shaped pattern in the variations with social class has also been found in national statistics (General Register Office, 1966).

A somewhat similar picture emerges when those who had two children were asked if they hoped they would have any more children. This can be seen from Table 66.

TABLE 66 Social class and hopes for further children among mothers with two children

	Social class of baby's father's occupation							All mothers
	I	II	III N	III M	IV	V	Unclassified	
	%	%	%	%	%	%	%	%
Yes	21	16	8	23	29	31	17	22
Uncertain	21	28	13	11	10	6	12	14
No, but might change mind	32	25	32	26	16	16	25	24
No, will not change mind	26	31	47	40	45	47	46	40
No. of mothers (= 100%)	34	83	40	201	87	32	24	501

Again, those in Social Class III non-manual were the ones least likely to want further children. Those in IV and V most often said they would like more children and few of them said they were uncertain or did not want more but might change their mind, whereas those in Classes I and II quite often said this. One possible explanation is that the middle-class mothers had a longer time perspective than the working-class mothers, and took into account more possible changes. Rather more middle- than working-class mothers said they might change their mind or decide to have further children if anything happened to their present children, 20% compared with 9%.

Working-class mothers more often gave housing as a reason for not wanting further children, 7% against 2%, and more of them said housing was a factor which affected the number they decided to have, 9% against 3%. There was no difference between middle- and working-class mothers in the proportion mentioning cost or expense as a reason for determining their family size.

It seemed that one reason for the higher proportion of working-class mothers with two children who wanted another was a greater desire for a mixed-sex family. There was no difference between middle- and working-class mothers among those who already had a boy and a girl in the proportion hoping for further children but among those with two children of the same sex 15% of middle-class mothers compared with 32% of those in the working-class wanted another.

One other significant class difference in their perceptions about the reasons why they did not want further children was that more of the middle- than of the working-class mothers mentioned their own or their husband's age, 15% compared with 8%. Middle-class mothers were appreciably older than working-class ones, the proportion aged 25 or more fell from 75% of the wives of professionals to 37% of the wives of men in unskilled jobs. This is partly because working-class women tend to marry earlier.

AGE AT MARRIAGE AND AGE AT FIRST PREGNANCY

The variation of age at marriage with social class is not U or J shaped but linear. The proportion of mothers in the sample who married in their teens rose from 14% of those with husbands in professional jobs to 58% of those with husbands in unskilled occupations. The pattern was similar for age at first pregnancy and for age at birth of the study baby. These variations are shown in Table 67.

TABLE 67 Social class and age at marriage, age at first pregnancy and age at birth of study baby

	Social class							All mothers
Mother's age at marriage:	I	II	III N	III M	IV	V	Unclas-sified	
	%	%	%	%	%	%	%	%
Under 20	14	23	30	43	42	58	39	38
20-24	65	61	52	48	48	32	57	50
25-29	17	11	16	7	8	5	4	9
30-34	4	4	}2	2	1	4	-	2
35 or over	-	1		-	1	1	-	1
Mother's age at first pregnancy:	%	%	%	%	%	%	%	%
Under 20	5	13	18	26	28	52	25	24
20-24	37	52	44	54	53	38	59	50
25-29	45	28	31	17	17	9	13	21
30-34	12	6	7	2	2	-	}3	4
35 or over	1	1	-	1	-	1		1
Mother's age at birth of study baby:	%	%	%	%	%	%	%	%
Under 20	-	5	5	11	9	27	10	10
20-24	25	32	30	39	43	36	47	37
25-29	38	42	44	33	25	22	30	33
30-34	23	15	16	12	16	10	6	14
35 or over	14	6	5	5	7	5	7	6
No. of mothers (=100%)*	93	201	131	615	250	116	67	1,473

* Small numbers for whom inadequate information was obtained have been omitted when the percentages were calculated.

One difficulty in interpreting these data is that social class
may change with age and in particular men may become professionals
at a later age or stage in their careers. So some mothers who
marry and have a baby when they are young may be included in the
study before their husbands became professionals. (Students are
counted as 'unclassified'.) This problem is less likely to affect
those in other social classes and while it may accentuate the
difference between professionals and others it seems unlikely to
account for the general trend.

Earlier (p.41) it was shown that the relationship between age at
first pregnancy and all the four measures of family size was linear,
they all decreased with increasing age at first pregnancy. In
addition, among those with two children, the proportion who hoped
they would have further children fell from 34% of those who had
their first pregnancy when they were in their teens to 13% of those
who did not start their family until they were 25 or more.

In terms of illuminating the relationship between social class
and family size, the age at which mothers have their first pregnancy
contributes to the increase in family size from those in skilled
non-manual jobs to those in unskilled jobs. It does not explain,
and to some extent makes the relatively large family size of those
in Social Classes I and II less understandable.

EDUCATION

One suggestion for the large family sizes of the professionals is
'that the (presumably) highly-educated wives of the self-employed
professional husbands suffer high opportunity costs in not working
and offset this loss with a deliberately high family (size)'
(Hawthorn, 1970, p.85).

The relationship between the social class of the father's
occupation and the mother's and father's education is shown in
Table 68.

Clearly social class is strongly related to the further education
and schooling of both mother and father. Again the relationship is
linear rather than U or J shaped.

Taking mother's further education, Table 69 shows that those with
no further education had the most number of children already - an
average of 2.06 compared with 1.79 among other mothers. (Census
data in 1961 showed fairly clear trends in fertility with duration
of mother's education, those with an early terminal age of education
having the highest fertility; General Register Office, 1966.) Those
with a university or polytechnic education had the smallest number -
but their average did not differ significantly from those with other
types of further education: 1.65 against 1.81. Looking at their
intended family size, again, those with no further education wanted
more children than other mothers. Among those with some further
education those who had trained as nurses wanted more children,
2.75 compared with 2.47 for those with other types of further
education.

These variations with mother's education cannot account for the
high family size of Social Class I. Mothers with a nursing training
were no more or less likely than other mothers with some further
education to be married to men in professional occupations.

TABLE 68   Social class and education

	Social class of baby's father's occupation							All mothers
	I	II	III N	III M	IV	V	Unclas- sified	
Mother's schooling:	%	%	%	%	%	%	%	%
Left as soon as old enough	30	42	67	77	78	81	60	68
Stayed on but no '0' or 'A' levels	11	14	11	10	14	11	20	12
'0' levels	24	27	15	11	6	8	15	13
'A' levels	35	17	7	2	2	–	5	7
Mother's further education:	%	%	%	%	%	%	%	%
University or polytechnic	18	7	3	1	2	1	3	3
Other	59	56	50	32	21	21	39	36
None	23	37	47	67	77	78	58	61
Father's schooling:	%	%	%	%	%	%	%	%
Left as soon as old enough	11	41	48	86	88	95	72	73
Stayed on but no '0' or 'A' levels	10	5	5	7	6	3	6	6
'0' levels	23	23	31	6	5	2	14	11
'A' levels	56	31	16	1	1	–	8	10
Father's further education:	%	%	%	%	%	%	%	%
University or polytechnic	53	21	6	3	1	–	9	8
Other	42	50	57	51	25	21	65	45
None	5	29	37	46	74	79	26	47
No. of mothers (= 100%)	93	201	131	615	250	116	67	1,473

TABLE 69 Mother's further education and family size

	Mother's further education						
	University or Polytechnic	Training College	Nursing	Technical college	Secretarial	Other	None
Average number of children at time of interview	1.65	1.68	2.00	1.67	1.81	1.87	2.06
Average number of intended children	2.52	2.45	2.75	2.51	2.45	2.47	2.62
No. of mothers	48	59	68	106	146	152	889

SOCIAL CLASS AND CONTRACEPTIVE EFFICIENCY

Another suggestion put forward by Hawthorn to explain the U or J shaped curve of fertility with social class is that the personal security afforded by the higher relative income induces relatively inefficient contraceptive practice.   This hypothesis appears initially to have some validity.   In Chapter 5 it was shown that Social Class I mothers were least likely to be taking the pill. Taking the proportion of mothers using no method or relatively unreliable methods (withdrawal, the safe period, or chemicals on their own) the variation with social class looks U or J shaped. It falls from 23% of those in Social Class I to 16% of those in Social Class III non-manual then rises to 27% of those in Social Class V, but the first of these differences might have occurred by chance.

If the wives of professional men had been using less efficient methods of contraception because they felt secure and therefore did not mind too much whether or not they had an additional pregnancy, they would be expected to have a higher proportion of unintended pregnancies but not a higher proportion of ones which they regretted, or felt 'sorry it happened at all'.

The figures in Table 70 show that only one of these predictions is borne out.   The proportion who felt 'sorry it happened at all' when they first found out about their last pregnancy was lowest, 8%, for those in Social Class I and rose to 19% of those in Social Class V. But the mothers in Social Class I were also the ones most likely to say their pregnancy was intended and this proportion dropped from three-quarters of them to half of mothers with husbands in unskilled jobs. There were no significant differences in the proportions who said they became pregnant while using some method of birth control. Nor were there any class differences in the proportions saying they sometimes took a chance and did not always use contraception.

TABLE 70   Social class and attitudes to last pregnancy

	Social class							All mothers
	I	II	III N	III M	IV	V	Unclas- sified	
Pregnancy intended:	%	%	%	%	%	%	%	%
Yes	76	73	68	64	60	51	61	65
No	24	27	32	36	40	49	39	35
Attitude:	%	%	%	%	%	%	%	%
Pleased	63	70	60	61	62	57	57	63
Rather earlier	16	11	15	10	9	3	10	10
Rather later	13	8	15	15	14	21	17	14
Sorry it happened at all	8	11	10	14	15	19	16	13
Using method of birth control:	%	%	%	%	%	%	%	%
Yes	16	20	21	23	22	20	25	22
No	84	80	79	77	78	80	75	78
No. of mothers (= 100%)	93	201	131	615	250	116	67	1,473

Further evidence that mothers in Social Class I did not have their comparatively large families unintentionally, or because they were using relatively inefficient contraception, comes from the question about the number of children they said they wanted at the time of their marriage.   Among those stating a number (those who said 'two or three' have been included at 2.5) the only social class group that stood out was I.   These mothers said they had wanted an average of 2.74 children compared with 2.32 for others. The other significant finding related to the proportion who said they had wanted some children but had no idea how many.   This was higher, 25%, for those in Social Classes IV and V than for other mothers, 17%.   Askham postulated that if the lower working class tend not to consider the future, one would not expect them to formulate in advance any definite preferences for the number of children they wanted to have (Askham, 1975).   Her findings did not support this but the figures on this study do.

Contraceptive inefficiency seems a more plausible explanation for the relatively large family sizes in Social Classes IV and V. They were more likely than wives of skilled manual workers to have unintended pregnancies and they were less likely to be using reliable methods of contraception.   (Sterilization, the pill, IUD, cap and sheath have been taken as reliable methods.)   Although they were no less likely to be taking the pill around the time of interview, there were a number of indications that they found it a somewhat less satisfactory method of birth control and therefore might not continue to take it for long.   They were more likely to report symptoms which they associated with the pill, less likely to say it was a very satisfactory method of contraception, and less likely to think it was very reliable.   There were, however, no class differences in the proportion regarding the pill as pleasant and easy to use or safe from the point of view of health (see Table 71).

TABLE 71 Social class and views of mothers taking the pill

	Middle class Social Class I, II & IIIN	Skilled manual IIIM	Partly and unskilled IV & V
Proportion with symptoms associated with pill at time of interview	19%	18%	28%
Proportion regarding pill as a 'very satisfactory' method on balance	81%	79%	66%
Proportion describing pill as 'very reliable'	92%	83%	76%
Proportion thinking pill quite safe to use from point of view of health	66%	73%	68%
Proportion describing pill as pleasant and easy to use	97%	96%	96%
Number of mothers taking pill (=100%)	183	289	166

One problem in the interpretation of these findings is that middle-class mothers had been taking the pill for rather longer. The proportion who first started taking the pill since their last baby was 34% of the middle-class mothers who were currently taking it, 44% among the wives of skilled manual workers and 57% among those in Social Classes IV and V.   These variations are related to their age differences, but still exist within age groups. Among mothers under 25, a third of the middle-class pill takers had started to take the pill after the survey baby was born compared with almost half, 45%, of working-class pill takers, and the comparable proportions among those aged 25-29 were 12% of the middle-class, 30% of the working-class.   So as a group, working-class mothers have a shorter experience of the pill.

The other clear trend that emerges from the analysis of attitudes to pregnancy (Table 70) is in the proportion of mothers who would have preferred their last pregnancy to be earlier.   This was 16% among Social Class I and 3% in Social Class V.   Is this because middle-class and working-class mothers have different views or experiences about spacing?

SOCIAL CLASS AND SPACING

Middle-class mothers less often than working-class ones said they felt it was appropriate to start a family straight away after marriage. ('Some people like to start a family straight away when they get married and others to leave it for a while. How do you feel about this?') This can be seen from Table 72, which also shows that the proportion who had their first baby within eight months of their marriage rose from 10% of Social Class I mothers to 43% of those in Social Class V. In addition, if those who must have been pregnant when they were married are excluded, middle-class women still postpone their first pregnancy for longer.

TABLE 72   Social class and intervals between marriage and first pregnancy

	Social class of baby's father's occupation							All mothers
	I	II	III N	III M	IV	V	Unclas-sified	
After marriage prefer to start family:	%	%	%	%	%	%	%	%
Straight away	22	22	23	30	33	35	25	28
Leave it a while	76	69	67	62	57	55	69	64
Other comment	2	9	10	8	10	10	6	8
Proportion whose first baby born within 8 months of marriage	10%	14%	18%	28%	27%	43%	22%	25%
Interval between marriage and first birth - excluding pre-marital conceptions:	%	%	%	%	%	%	%	%
8 months < 1 year	12	15	12	20	27	27	19	19
1 year < 2 years	35	31	29	36	32	46	48	36
2 years < 3 years	20	20	24	20	23	16	13	20
3 years < 4 years	13	16	14	10	11	9	4	11
4 years < 5 years	7	10	12	6	2	-	10	6
5 years or longer	13	8	9	8	5	2	6	8
No. of mothers (=100%): Total	93	201	131	615	250	116	67	1,473
: Excluding pre-marital conc.	83	168	107	428	172	55	52	1,065

Since social class is so strongly related to age at marriage and, as shown in Chapter 4, age at marriage seemed to influence spacing patterns and views, a three-way analysis is needed to sort out these relationships. Table 73 shows that both social class and age at marriage are related independently to mothers' views and experiences of the interval between marriage and starting a family.

TABLE 73   Social class, age at marriage and spacing

	Age at marriage		
	Under 20	20-24	25 or over
Proportion preferring to start family straight away			
Middle class	28% (98)	18% (248)	29% (75)
Working class	34% (426)	27% (445)	39% (92)
Proportion whose first baby born within 8 months of marriage			
Middle class	29% (98)	10% (248)	9% (76)
Working class	45% (428)	17% (447)	20% (92)
Proportion whose first baby born within 1 year of marriage - excluding premarital conceptions			
Middle class	16% (67)	13% (222)	13% (68)
Working class	24% (221)	19% (355)	31% (70)

Working-class mothers were more apt than middle-class mothers both to prefer to start their family straight away, and to do that. This difference held whether they were married before they were 20 or in their early twenties.

The only class difference in the actual space between the last two children was in the proportion for which it was less than a year, 3% of working-class mothers, less than 1% of middle-class.

SOCIAL CLASS AND JOBS

One job characteristic that was strongly related to social class and might have some bearing on decisions about family size was whether or not the father had a chance of getting a better job. ('Would you say that in his line of work, he has a chance of getting a better job or not?') Altogether two-thirds of the mothers thought their husbands were in jobs where they might get a better one, and this proportion was 83% of middle-class mothers, 61% of those with husbands in skilled manual jobs, 51% of those in partly skilled and 45% of those in unskilled. It did not vary significantly with the husband's age.   The ways in which this related to their present and their intended family size are shown in Table 74.

The differences are hard to interpret.   It would seem that, apart from those in Social Class V, those who felt they had a chance of a better job had fewer children at the time of the study than those who did not have such prospects.   In relation to average intended family size only two of the four differences were significant and they were in opposite directions.   Among mothers with husbands in unskilled jobs, the chance of a better job seems to be related with an increase in family size intentions.   Other studies have also related perceptions of job opportunities to fertility

(Westoff et al., 1961, pp.249-50; Westoff et al., 1963, pp.140-4).
They conclude that 'all in all, the results continue to discourage
any conclusion other than that social mobility as measured has at
best a trivial statistical association with fertility' (Westoff
et al., 1963, p.147).

TABLE 74   Social class, family size and better job chances

| | Average present family size | | Significance of difference |
	Those with chance of better job	Those without chance of a better job	
Middle class	1.79 (345)	2.05 (62)	*
Skilled manual	1.83 (363)	2.06 (209)	**
Partly skilled	1.92 (120)	2.48 (108)	****
Unskilled	2.09 (46)	1.87 (54)	-
	Average intended family size		
Middle class	2.49 (336)	2.65 (61)	-
Skilled manual	2.57 (359)	2.55 (207)	-
Partly skilled	2.50 (120)	2.90 (107)	***
Unskilled	2.98 (46)	2.33 (53)	***

    * p<.05
   ** p<.02
  *** p<.01
 **** p<.001

   Whether or not the mother was working around the time of interview was unrelated to the social class of her husband's occupation,
although more working-class than middle-class mothers said they
approved of mothers working. (Eight per cent of working-class
mothers, 5% of middle-class ones said they approved of women working
if they had children under school age, 31% and 43% respectively if
they had children of school age.)   Altogether 3% were working
full-time and 9% part-time.   However, these proportions varied with
the social class of the woman's own occupation (her present or last
full-time occupation has been used for this).   The proportion
working was over half of the few (12) in professional jobs, a fifth
of those in intermediate occupations, and a tenth of the others.
But the average number of children mothers intended to have was
similar for those who were working at the time of the interview and
those who were not.   So too was the average number they already had.
   The relationship between the social class of the mother's
occupation and her present and intended family size only showed
significant differences between those in manual and non-manual
occupations.   Mothers whose present or last full-time job was non-
manual had, and wanted, fewer children than those with manual ones.
Those who had never had a full-time job had and wanted the largest
families. (IF NOT WORKING NOW, 'Do you think you will go (back) to
work ever?')   The averages were:

	Non-manual	Manual	No full- time job
At time of interview	1.77 (829)	2.13 (534)	2.65 (78)
Intended	2.47 (811)	2.65 (526)	3.22 (77)

A study in North America also found that women who had never worked expected and wanted larger families (Ryder and Westoff, 1971, pp.61-3).   In that study, covering much larger numbers of women who were currently working, women who were working expected to have fewer children.   A further indication that mothers who did not work were likely to have larger families came from a question about whether they thought they would go back to work. (The majority of them, three-quarters, had had no further education and half had married before they were 20.)   Those who said not, intended to have an average of 2.83 children while those who were not working at the time of interview but planned to do so later wanted an average of 2.52.

The social class distribution of the mothers' jobs was quite different from that of their husbands.   Almost half had had skilled non-manual jobs, a quarter partly skilled ones, one in eight had had skilled manual jobs, and another one in eight intermediate occupations.   Very few were at the two extremes.   This can be seen from Table 75, which also shows the relationship between the social class of mothers' and fathers' jobs.

TABLE 75   Relationship between the social class of mothers' and fathers' jobs

Social class of mothers' present or last full-time occupation	Social class of father's occupation							All mothers
	I	II	III N	III M	IV	V	Unclas-sified	
	%	%	%	%	%	%	%	%
I Professional	8	2	-	-	-	-	-	1
II Intermediate	34	32	15	5	6	3	16	12
III Skilled								
non-manual	41	48	54	50	35	31	42	44
manual	3	6	11	13	13	18	14	12
IV Partly skilled	8	9	15	27	33	38	17	24
V Unskilled	1	-	2	1	2	3	-	1
No full-time occupation	5	3	3	4	11	7	11	6
No. of mothers (=100%)	92	198	131	607	241	112	63	1,444

THE QUESTIONS THAT HAVE BEEN RAISED

At the beginning of this chapter it was recognized that these analyses would raise issues and not provide explanations.   In trying to understand something about the differences in desired and achieved family size, two approaches have been made.

One approach was to try to see why mothers with husbands in
partly skilled and unskilled occupations had and wanted relatively
large families.   A number of clues were picked up.   One was that
they did not appear to have wanted a particularly large family size
at the time of their marriage, but a relatively high proportion
said that at that point in time they did not have clear ideas about
the number of children they hoped to have.   Askham has suggested
that the lower working class have orientations towards the future
and towards individuals' control over their own lives which may be
relevant here.   She quotes data from a number of other studies
(Rainwater, 1960, p.57; Cohen and Hodges, 1963; Schneiderman,
1964) besides her own and reasons that 'Lower working class groups
tend to have a present rather than a future time orientation because
for them the future is more uncertain and insecure than it is for
other social groups ... their goals will be for present rather than
future gratification.'   She also sees the lower working class as
being 'unable to control the major events of their own lives because
they are socially and economically deprived, and their command over
resources is minimal' (Askham, 1975).   These two orientations seem
helpful in understanding another observation that mothers in Social
Classes IV and V were less effective users of contraception than
other mothers: they tended to use rather less effective methods
and to have more unintended pregnancies.   Another mechanism that
plays a part is age at marriage and age at first pregnancy.   Mothers
with husbands in unskilled occupations were particularly likely to
marry and have their first baby before they were 20.   This may stem
in part from leaving school early, and the sort of jobs they go into,
and in part from their concern with the present rather than the
future.
    The other approach was to look at possible reasons why mothers
with husbands in professional occupations both have and want
relatively large families.   Variables that were explored for
possible clues were mother's education, use of contraception, age at
marriage, likelihood of the father getting a better job, and the
mother's work.   It did not appear that any of these variables
helped to explain this observation.   Neither did the reasons given
by the mothers for their choices vary with the social class in ways
that threw much light on the difference.   But since financial
considerations loomed so large in the reasons given by mothers of
all social classes, and the families of professionals tend to be
better off than others, there may be some hidden clues here.   These
will be searched for in a later chapter.   One reason for limiting
family size which was mentioned rather more often by working-class
mothers was housing.   This is looked at next.

Chapter 11

HOUSING AND POPULATION PRESSURES

Relatively few mothers mentioned either housing conditions or population pressures as factors which contributed to their decision-making on family size.   Yet there have been quite dramatic changes recently in home ownership and in public discussion and awareness of population problems and pressures.   It is tempting to try and link these with the recent fall in the birth rate.   This chapter looks at the evidence for such links.

HOUSING TRENDS

Between 1950 and 1960 the ownership of dwellings in the United Kingdom altered dramatically.   The proportion of dwellings rented from local authorities or new towns and the proportion of owner-occupied dwellings both increased by about 50% while the proportion rented from private owners fell from 45% to 26%.   Between 1960 and 1973 the same trends have continued, but at a lower rate.   This can be seen from Table 76.

TABLE 76   Trends in the ownership of dwellings in the United Kingdom

	1950	1960	1970	1973
	%	%	%	%
Owner-occupied	29	42	50	52
Rented from local authorities or new towns	18	26	30	31
Rented from private owners	45	26	15	17
Other tenures	8	6	5	
Number of dwellings (000's)	*	16,600	19,183	19,891

Source: Central Statistical Office, 'Social Trends', no.5,
         pp.161-2.
* Not given

One obstacle in seeing these trends as possibly contributing to the fall in the birth rate is that the main changes preceded the steepest fall in the birth rate. However, the impact of overall changes in home ownership may not be felt by couples with young families for a number of years.

Table 77 shows how home ownership varied between mothers of different ages.

TABLE 77 Age and home ownership

	Mother's age					All mothers
	Under 20	20-24	25-29	30-34	35 or more	
	%	%	%	%	%	%
Owned on mortgage	13	36	57	56	44	44
Owned outright	3	2	4	5	6	4
Rented from Council	37	32	23	25	37	29
Rented privately unfurnished	21	15	9	7	5	12
Rented privately furnished	12	5	2	1	3	4
Tied	6	4	2	3	3	3
Other	8	6	3	3	2	4
No. of mothers (=100%)	146	544	484	201	87	1,472

The proportion buying their home on a mortgage rose from one in eight of those under 20 to over half those aged 25-34; it then dropped somewhat for the older mothers. This drop might reflect a generation difference - women born before 1940 may be less likely to buy a house at any stage in their lives than those born more recently - or it may be that women having a baby relatively late differ in other ways which in turn are related to home ownership.

HOUSING AND FAMILY SIZE

If increasing home ownership has played any part in the falling birth rate it needs to be shown that couples who are buying their houses have relatively small families. The data are in Table 78.

Comparing the two main groups, those buying their homes on a mortgage and those renting it from a Council (72% of the mothers were in one of these two categories), Council tenants had and wanted the larger number of children. This may be partly because it is easier for larger families to get a Council home. But couples with a mortgage may feel somewhat less inclined to take on further responsibilities in the form of a larger family. Those who were buying their home on a mortgage had and wanted fewer children than those who owned their homes outright.

TABLE 78 Home ownership and family size

Average number of children:	Type of housing: Owned on mortgage	Owned outright	Rented from Council	Rented privately unfurnished	Rented privately furnished	Tied	Other	All mothers
At time of interview	1.85	2.25	2.31	1.76	1.48	1.92	1.60	1.96
At time of interview by those not wanting more	2.44	2.61	2.77	2.27	*	2.52	2.10	2.54
Wanted altogether by those wanting more or uncertain	2.51	3.04	2.86	2.51	2.50	2.60	2.73	2.64
Intended	2.48	2.84	2.81	2.42	2.47	2.56	2.52	2.58
No. of mothers:								
Not wanting more	290	23	237	66	16	25	20	677
Wanting more or uncertain	346	26	179	107	45	24	40	769
Total	646	52	421	175	62	51	65	1,473

* Numbers too small.

Council tenants were less often middle-class than people buying their houses on a mortgage: 13% against 44% had husbands in non-manual occupations. But it seemed that the apparent 'effects' of both social class and type of housing existed independently.

The data in Table 79 show that among those with a mortgage there were little or no class differences in their family intentions, but class differences persisted among Council tenants. Differences between Council tenants and those buying their home existed between working-class but not middle-class mothers. Middle-class families in Council housing seem to retain their middle-class aspirations in relation to family size, and do not appear to be Council tenants because they have large families. But people in manual occupations who take out a mortgage also seem to have the family size aspirations of other middle-class people who are buying their homes. Possibly some of them buy a house because they have accepted middle-class values.

An indication that buying a house on a mortgage may influence people's intentions about family size comes from an analysis of the number of children they said they wanted at the time of their marriage. At that stage there was no significant difference between the number wanted by mothers who, at the time of interview, were

Council tenants and those who were buying their homes. But it may be that later on those who for one reason or other had had more children were more able to get a Council tenancy while those who had smaller families were more able to afford a mortgage.

TABLE 79   Social class, house ownership and family size

	Average number of children			
	At time of interview		Intended	
Social class	Mortgage	Council	Mortgage	Council
I Professional	1.93 (76)	2.03 (31)	2.66 (74)	2.65 (31)
II Intermediate	1.80 (121)		2.44 (117)	
III Skilled:				
Non-manual	1.78 (79)	1.86 (22)	2.44 (78)	2.41 (22)
Manual	1.79 (254)	2.31 (205)	2.45 (252)	2.80 (202)
IV Partly skilled	1.94 (72)	2.48 (99)	2.43 (72)	2.93 (99)
V Unskilled	2.04 (23)	2.35 (54)	2.59 (23)	2.90 (53)
Middle class	1.83	1.96	2.50	2.55
Working class	1.84	2.37	2.46	2.85

HOUSING CONDITIONS

To what extent, if at all, do the amenities in different types of housing contribute to people's decisions about their family sizes? Table 80 shows the amenities of various types of accommodation.

Those who were buying their house on a mortgage were the ones most likely to have a garden and to live in a house rather than a flat.   They also had fewer persons per room and were most likely to feel their home was suitable for bringing up their present family. ('Would you say your house/flat is suitable for bringing up your present family?' IF YES, 'Would it still be suitable if you had another baby?')   Most of those who owned their homes outright also thought their home suitable for their family but, compared with buying their home on a mortgage, they had fewer amenities, less often had a garden, had less space and more often lived in a terrace house. Council house tenants were well off for amenities but had less space than the owner-occupiers and three-tenths of them lived in flats rather than a house.   Those living in privately rented accommodation, particularly those renting it furnished, were the least well off in terms of overcrowding and space.   They more often lived in flats and were least likely to regard their accommodation as suitable for their family.

TABLE 80   The amenities of different types of accommodation

	Type of accommodation							All types of accommodation
	Owned on mort-gage	Owned out-right	Rented from Coun-cil	Rented priv-ately unfur-nished	Rented priv-ately fur-nished	Tied	Other	
	%	%	%	%	%	%	%	%
Garden:								
Yes own	94	77	73	37	23	74	80	76
Yes shared	1	2	4	20	48	4	12	7
None	5	21	23	43	29	22	8	17
Proportion with indoor w.c., fixed bath and hot water tap	94%	71%	96%	56%	44%	90%	74%	86%
Persons per room:	%	%	%	%	%	%	%	%
Less than $\frac{3}{4}$	50	29	12	18	16	29	22	31
$\frac{3}{4} < 1$	31	31	30	31	13	41	20	30
1	11	17	34	33	26	24	23	22
Over 1 - $1\frac{1}{2}$	7	21	22	14	19	4	21	14
Over $1\frac{1}{2}$	1	2	2	4	26	2	14	3
Type of housing:	%	%	%	%	%	%	%	%
Detached house	18	15	-	10	2	10	16	11
Semi-detached	44	15	30	5	8	31	28	32
Terrace	36	64	40	34	15	31	42	37
Flat - purpose built	1	-	29	16	3	24	5	12
Flat - self-contained con-verted	-	2	1	15	21	4	3	3
Flat or rooms, not self-contained	-	-	-	18	49	-	6	4
Other	1	4	-	2	2	-	-	1
Suitable for family:	%	%	%	%	%	%	%	%
Yes - and if had another	66	62	37	23	20	52	31	48
Yes - at pres-ent	22	25	22	19	12	10	26	21
No	12	13	41	58	68	38	43	31
No. of mothers (= 100%)	646	52	421	175	62	51	65	1,473

   Table 81 shows that mothers were much less likely to regard a flat - as opposed to a house - as suitable for bringing up their family.   And the higher up the flat the smaller the proportion of mothers who felt it was suitable (see also Jephcott, 1971; Ineichen and Hooper, 1974).   Those who shared a garden were no more likely than those who had none at all to feel their home was suitable. There was a clear trend with the number of persons per room, and those who did not have an indoor w.c., a fixed bath and a hot water tap less often felt their home suitable, but even so, 43% of those without at least one of these amenities and 47% of those living with more than one person per room still regarded their home as suitable for bringing up their present family, so many mothers' expectations were modest.

TABLE 81 Variation in mothers' feelings about the suitability of their homes with different amenities

	Proportion feeling their home was suitable for bringing up their present family	Number of mothers (= 100%)
Garden:		
Yes - own	82%	1,121
Yes - shared	34%	96
None	33%	247
Indoor w.c., fixed bath and hot water tap:		
Yes	75%	1,264
No	43%	204
Persons per room:		
Less than $\frac{3}{4}$	92%	457
$\frac{3}{4}$ < 1	76%	442
1	52%	322
Over 1 - $1\frac{1}{2}$	51%	196
Over $1\frac{1}{2}$	30%	50
Type of housing:		
Detached house	90%	157
Semi-detached	86%	458
Terraced	74%	544
Flat - purpose built	31%	173
Flat - self-contained, converted	35%	48
Flat or rooms not self-contained	26%	65
Other or inadequate response	74%	23
Floor of flat:		
Ground	39%	46
First	35%	102
Second	28%	43
Third	25%	36
Fourth or higher	13%	32

Whether or not mothers regarded their present home as suitable for their family did not seem to be related to the total number of children they intended to have.   But, taking just mothers with two children, those who said their house or flat was suitable for bringing up their present family but would not be suitable if they had another baby were the ones least likely to want another child - 13% of them did so compared with 23% of those who felt their present home was not suitable and 24% of those who thought their present home would be suitable if they had another baby.   This suggests that 'intermediate' type of housing may be more of a restraint on having further children than housing which is either better or worse in terms of the mother's assessment of its suitability for bringing up a family.   But in terms of objective criteria, such as whether or not their home had three basic amenities (an indoor w.c., a fixed bath and a hot water tap), only 20% of mothers in homes with all three amenities wanted a third child compared with 38% of mothers without such facilities.   This did not appear to be a function of people wanting an extra child in the hope of getting a Council house or flat, since those living in privately rented accommodation were no more likely than those in Council homes to want a third child.   It appears to be another example of an experience of poverty and lack of material comforts being associated with higher family size (see Askham, 1975).

SOCIAL CLASS AND HOUSING

Associations between social class and housing, shown in Table 82, may help in understanding why wives of unskilled workers have and want larger families.   Once again, the relationships are linear and not U or J shaped.   But if there is a tendency for those in better and those in worse housing to want larger families than those in more average accommodation, this may contribute to the social class distribution on family size.
There are probably three ways in which housing might influence family size decisions - amenities, security, and economics.   First amenities, for which there was a clear social class gradient.   In addition to the ones in the Table the proportion with their own garden fell from 97% of those in Social Class I to 67% in V, while the proportion living in households with more than one person to a room rose from 6% to 27%.   But the evidence suggests that actual and intended family size was greater among those who lacked amenities.   Secondly, security.   This was probably least for those in privately rented furnished accommodation, and greatest among those buying their homes or living in Council accommodation.   Again there was a clear class gradient.   But since Council tenants and those with a mortgage had such different family size aspirations, it would not appear that housing security on its own played a large part in family size decisions.   Thirdly, economics.   Here the data (see Table 83) suggest that those living in rented accommodation, either from the Council or privately, saw themselves as less well off than other families they knew well and they more often thought their family incomes inadequate.   The associations between these attitudes and family size will be discussed in the next chapter.

TABLE 82   Social class and housing

	Social class of husband's occupation					
	I	II	III N	III M	IV	V
	%	%	%	%	%	%
Home ownership:						
Owned - on mortgage	83	61	59	41	29	20
Owned - outright	2	4	5	3	6	3
Rented from Council	6	12	17	33	39	45
Rented privately, unfurnished	3	15	9	13	12	15
Rented privately, furnished	1	1	1	4	4	11
Tied	2	3	4	2	4	3
Other	3	4	5	4	6	3
Indoor w.c., fixed bath and hot water tap:	%	%	%	%	%	%
Yes	97	94	91	86	82	70
No	3	6	9	14	18	30
Type of housing:	%	%	%	%	%	%
Detached	35	26	14	6	3	4
Semi-detached	43	34	37	32	24	20
Terraced	19	19	31	41	48	52
Flat - purpose built	2	12	10	12	16	10
Flat - self-contained, converted	1	5	5	3	4	3
Flat or rooms, not self-contained	-	2	2	5	5	10
Other	-	2	1	1	-	1
Suitable for family:	%	%	%	%	%	%
No	12	21	24	31	42	41
Yes, at present	21	25	21	22	16	26
Yes, if another baby	67	54	55	47	42	33
Number of mothers (= 100%)	93	201	131	615	250	116

TABLE 83   Housing and views on economic circumstances

	Type of housing						
	Owned on mort-gage	Owned out-right	Rented from Coun-cil	Rented priv-ately unfur-nished	Rented priv-ately fur-nished	Tied	Other
Family income felt to be:	%	%	%	%	%	%	%
Enough for needs	76	84	59	61	67	75	67
More than enough	8	2	7	9	3	-	8
Less than enough	16	14	34	30	30	25	25
Saves money:	%	%	%	%	%	%	%
Yes	76	80	65	76	63	72	77
No	24	20	35	24	37	28	23
Compared with other families knows well:	%	%	%	%	%	%	%
Mother better off	30	25	22	20	16	25	17
Same	62	67	66	68	66	63	59
Mother worse off	5	4	10	10	13	8	16
Other comment	3	4	2	2	5	4	8
In five years expects to be:	%	%	%	%	%	%	%
Better off	65	59	57	66	66	65	61
Same	29	31	33	26	26	29	31
Worse off	5	6	9	7	5	4	3
Other comment	1	4	1	1	3	2	5
No. of mothers (= 100%)	646	52	421	175	62	51	64

   Altogether variations with the types of homes in which people live have illustrated the complexity of family size decision-making rather than identified reasons for a fall in the birth rate.   Are their perceptions of and reactions to population pressures more illuminating?

POPULATION

Discussion about population problems and pressures has become frequent and popular.   1974 was designated World Population Year by the World Health Organization, and there was a Population Day on 12 May 1973, in the middle of the interviewing for this study.
   With this escalation of discussion it seemed worth finding out what proportion of parents thought there was a population problem in this country and, for those who felt there was one, whether they

perceived it as relevant to their decisions about family size.

Two-thirds of the mothers thought there was a population problem in this country, a sixth thought there was not, and a sixth were uncertain.   Those who thought there was or were uncertain were asked first whether they thought people should not have more than a certain number of children because of this, and if so, whether they thought it had or might make a difference to the number of children they have.   Altogether 44% of the mothers thought people ought to restrict their number of children because of the population problem, and 20% thought this consideration had or might make a difference to the number of children they had.

Two questions seem worth pursuing.   First, what sort of people perceive a population problem, and secondly is there any indication that perception of a problem affects action and intentions.

PERCEPTION OF A PROBLEM

Two basic hypotheses were looked at here.   First that those who perceived a population problem would be better educated, more middle-class than those who did not.   That is, their perception of the problem would result from education, reading, or discussion, and their awareness of other people's problems rather than by direct observation.

The second hypothesis was that those who lived in overcrowded conditions had no garden, lived in the town rather than the country, in the South-East rather than the North, would respond to such conditions by perceiving a population problem.

To some extent these hypotheses are likely to be confounded in that people with more education, and those who are better off, who by the first hypothesis are likely to be more aware of a population problem, are also those least likely to live in overcrowded conditions and therefore by the second hypothesis will be less aware of population pressures.

Taking the first hypothesis first, there was no indication that perception of a population problem was related to social class but it did appear to be related to education.   This is shown in Table 84.

The difference with education are not large but they are in the predicted direction whereas variations in overcrowding, as measured by the number of persons per room, went in the opposite direction to that predicted by the second hypothesis.   The more overcrowded people, with more persons per room, were less likely to think there was a population problem than those who lived in households with fewer people per room.   In addition, husbands and wives who shared their home with people other than just themselves and their children less often thought there was a population problem than those who lived in a 'nuclear' family of mother, father, and children only. But a high proportion of the small group who lived in a house or flat that was owned by their parent or parent-in-law thought there was a population problem.   Those who owned their own house more often perceived a population problem than those who lived in a Council house or flat.   There were no clear-cut differences with the type of housing although those living in a detached house seemed more likely to consider there was a population problem than those living in a terraced house. These results are in Table 85.

TABLE 84 Variations in perceptions of a population problem with education and lack of variation with social class

	Proportion thinking there is a popula- tion problem in this country	Number of mothers (= 100%)
Schooling:		
Left school as soon as possible	65%	981
Stayed on but did not take '0' or 'A' levels	64%	171
Took '0' level exams - but not 'A' levels	70%	196
Took 'A' level exams	76%	97
Further education:		
University or polytechnic	79%	48
Other	67%	530
None	64%	883
Social class:		
I Professional	65%	93
II Intermediate	71%	201
III Skilled non-manual	65%	131
III Skilled manual	65%	610
IV Semi-skilled	61%	248
V Unskilled	67%	115

TABLE 85 Variations in perceptions of a population problem with housing circumstance

	Proportion thinking there is a popula- tion problem in this country	Number of mothers (= 100%)
Persons per room:		
Less than $\frac{1}{2}$	87%	23
$\frac{1}{2} < \frac{3}{4}$	66%	433
$\frac{3}{4} < 1$	70%	443
1	67%	321
Over 1 up to $1\frac{1}{2}$	57%	194
Over $1\frac{1}{2}$	53%	49
Household composition:		
Father, mother & children only	67%	1,293
Father, mother, children & others	58%	148
Housing ownership:		
Own or on mortgage	68%	714
Rent from Council	62%	420
Rent privately	65%	234
In house/flat owned by parents	82%	22
Tied	75%	51
Type of housing:		
Detached house	73%	158
Semi-detached	67%	458
Terrace house	63%	541
Self-contained flat or maisonette	67%	220
Flat or rooms - not self-contained	61%	64

Other data relating to the second hypothesis were the type of areas in which the family was living.   There was no difference between those in rural and other types of districts in the proportion who thought there was a population problem.   Those living in the North or in Wales (Maryport and Workington, Hull, Sheffield, Oldham, Tadcaster, Northumberland North, Clowne, and Llantrisant and Llantwit Fardre) were less likely to think there was a population problem than those living in London, the South, or the Midlands, 62% against 68%, but this and the small group living in accommodation owned by their parents was the only evidence in support of the second hypothesis. The other differences were in the opposite direction.

The conclusion then is that the people who believe there is a population problem in this country are the better educated and those living in better-off housing conditions.   The belief does not appear to be related to direct experience of overcrowding.

BELIEF AND ACTION

Among mothers with two children, those who thought there was a population problem were less likely to say they wanted more children than those who thought there was not.   The same association held for those with three children.   This is shown in Table 86.

TABLE 86   Association between perception of a population problem and hopes for further children among mothers with two and three children

	Mothers with 2 children			Mothers with 3 children		
	Do you think we have a population problem in this country?			Do you think we have a population problem in this country?		
Do you hope you will have any more children?	Yes	Uncertain	No	Yes	Uncertain	No
	%	%	%	%	%	%
Yes	18	21	37	9	6	23
Uncertain	37	49	33	28	32	26
No	45	30	30	63	62	51
Number of mothers (= 100%)	331	90	79	141	34	43

Views on a population problem were not related to preferences for a single-child family, nor were they associated with their wishes for further children if they already had four or more children.   But what influences people to have three rather than two children is one of the most fascinating and important things for demographers.   An association between views about a population problem and their intentions is suggestive, but of course it may be that whether or not they want a larger family affects their perceptions about a population problem rather than the other way round.

Further evidence of the association between attitudes to population problems and intentions comes from data about intended family size.   The average number of children intended was 2.32 among those who thought the population problem had or might make a difference to the number of children they had, and 2.65 among the others.   The average numbers they already had were 1.77 and 2.00 respectively.

To sum up, the differences observed certainly do not contradict the hypothesis that an increase in the perception of a population problem may lead to reduction in family size.   But more evidence would be needed before the hypothesis can be accepted.   If the hypothesis is valid, the effect may well increase since perception of a population problem is higher among the more educated and the better housed.   It is not, however, greatly influenced by such transitory measures as 'population day' in 1973.   The proportion who thought there was a population problem in this country was 67% among those interviewed on or before 12 May, 65% among those interviewed afterwards.

Chapter 12

ECONOMIC INFLUENCES

Economic considerations were the reasons most commonly given by mothers for not wanting further children or for choosing a partic- ular family size.   At the same time it has been shown that it is the wives of partly skilled and unskilled workers, who are likely to be the least well off materially, who have and want comparatively large families.   There has been much discussion and a number of studies about the ways in which income levels and people's attitudes towards them may influence fertility.   Feelings of relative wealth or deprivation may be as relevant as, or more relevant than, absolute levels of income; expectations about future changes, variations in people's desire for material goods and for education, and the 'opportunity costs' to wives of raising children, are all likely to influence family size.

No attempt is made here to contribute to the discussion on appropriate models or the appropriateness of models.   This chapter presents some straightforward data about a few economic factors which may be related to fertility.   In addition, mothers' views and plans about working and their husbands' experience of unemploy- ment are looked at.

No questions were asked about actual incomes on this study because the value of the information did not seem likely to be worth the problems of obtaining it.   It is difficult to collect adequate data without asking many questions, and this may antagonize people and increase failure and refusal rates.   It seemed more useful to ask people their attitudes to their income - how they saw it in relation to their needs, how it compared with the income of other families they knew well, how they felt their economic situation had changed in the past and was likely to change in the future.

ATTITUDES TO INCOME

Most mothers, 69%, thought their family income was enough for their needs, 7% rated it more than enough, and 24% as less than they needed. ('How would you rate your family income at the moment - would you say it was enough for your needs, more than enough, or less than you really need?')   And when they were asked to compare themselves with families they knew well and who were about the same age as them a quarter reckoned that they and their husbands were better off, only one in twelve that they were worse off. ('Compared with families you know well who are about the same age as you and your husband, would you say you were better off financially, worse off, or about the same as them?')   Replies to both these questions were clearly related to social class.   Just over a third of the wives of unskilled workers reckoned their family income was less than they needed.   But it is clear from the figures in Table 87 that feelings about their income were by no means solely determined by their social class.   The similarities between classes are in some ways more striking than the differences.

TABLE 87   Social class and attitudes to income

	Social class							All mothers
	I	II	III N	III M	IV	V	Unclas- sified	
Income :	%	%	%	%	%	%	%	%
Enough	81	75	74	67	63	59	72	69
More than enough	9	7	8	9	3	5	9	7
Less than needed	10	18	18	24	34	36	19	24
Compared with other families she knows well mother feels:	%	%	%	%	%	%	%	%
Better off	34	30	24	25	21	19	23	25
Same	52	57	64	67	63	67	67	64
Worse off	5	9	11	5	13	12	6	8
Other comment	9	4	1	3	3	2	4	3
Number of mothers (= 100%)	93	201	131	615	250	116	67	1,473

Feelings about the adequacy of their income and whether they were better off than other couples they knew well were closely related. The proportion who thought they were well off compared with other couples they knew was 57% among those who felt their income was more than enough for their needs, 26% among those who described it as enough, and 12% among those who said it was less than they needed.

Mothers who thought their income was more than enough for their needs had fewer children than those who thought their income was enough, and those who found it less than enough had the largest families.   A similar trend was observed for the number of children they wanted altogether (see Table 88).

The differences in the number of children they already had persisted within social class groups, and reflect the fact that mothers with larger families were less likely to feel their incomes were adequate.   But taking just those with two children, the proportion wanting another child was 14% of those who felt their income was more than enough, 20% of those who felt it was enough, and 28% of those who regarded it as less than they needed.   It may be that some mothers felt their income was not enough for their needs because they wanted a third child, even though they were asked to rate their family income 'at the moment'.   No consistent association was found between family size and mothers' feelings about whether they were better or worse off than other families they knew.

TABLE 88   Attitudes to income and family size

| | Views on income | | |
Average number of children:	More than enough	Enough	Not enough
At time of interview	1.67	1.90	2.19
Intended	2.44	2.56	2.68
Number of mothers (= 100%)	106	1,001	356

It is difficult to make sense of these findings without being wildly speculative.   It may be that when mothers said they did not want more children, or only wanted two children because of the expense, this is more a reflection of cultural norms and expectations than of their own individual situation.   For various reasons they had decided they wanted two children and they perceived economic factors as influencing that decision, but there is no evidence from this study to show that economic pressures act in any direct way on individuals.   Further evidence of the small part played by an increase in income on increasing family size is given in the next section on affording children.

AFFORDING CHILDREN

To try and get some idea whether relatively small increases of income might affect people's views on the number of children they wanted, mothers were asked - 'If you had more money - say another £5 a week between you and your husband - what would you do with it?' Replies are shown in Table 89.   Only one mother thought she might have a larger family - 'I would like another baby.   I think we could afford another one then.'

TABLE 89   Ways in which mothers would spend extra £5 a week

	%
Save it (put in bank, invest)	50
New house/home	7
Things for house	18
Things for children or family	22
Food, housekeeping	13
Clothes	9
Holiday, leisure activities	7
Car	3
Would be swallowed up by increased prices, cost of living	2
Others	2
Number of mothers (= 100%)	1,444

Percentages add to more than 100 as some mothers gave more than one answer.

However, in response to a further question - 'Is there any chance that you might decide to have a larger family than you would otherwise have done - if you had another £5 a week?' - 4% of mothers said they might do this and another 2% were uncertain.   The proportion who might consider it rose from 1% of wives of professionals to 8% of the wives of unskilled workers.   The group who said they might decide to have a larger family if they had another £5 a week contained a relatively high proportion of mothers who wanted another child anyway, 61% compared with 45% of those who said this would not make any difference.   These findings suggest that a substantial increase in the family allowance would only have a very small effect on people's family size intentions.

The concept of babies as 'consumer durables' has been criticized by Blake because 'it fails to take into account important elements in the sociology of reproduction' (1968).   She argues that there is no purchase price for children, and that 'the poor seem to share in certain society-wide pro-natalist motivational pressures, but do not share in many of the anti-natalist ones affecting the middle and upper income groups in modern societies.'   But, as Busfield has pointed out, 'this lack of equivalence between children and consumer durables does not mean that in making decisions about family size, it is not generally believed that issues of cost and of what one can afford should play a part' (1974).   Certainly the mothers in this study were rather more prepared to answer the question about the number of children they could afford ('What is the largest number of children you think you can afford to bring up reasonably?') than one about the best number of children for couples more or less like themselves.   (Eight per cent of the mothers said they could not answer this, it was up to the couples to decide.)   The distribution by social class is shown in Table 90.

TABLE 90   Social class and the largest number of children mothers reckoned they could afford

	Social class							All mothers
	I	II	III N	III M	IV	V	Un-classified	
	%	%	%	%	%	%	%	%
One	1	4	5	2	2	3	-	2
One or two	1	-	-	1	1	2	-	1
Two	26	39	39	42	41	34	47	40
Two or three	3	5	6	3	2	2	2	3
Three	31	31	33	34	33	29	26	33
Three or four	2	2	2	1	2	5	3	2
Four	27 }36	16 }19	11 }15	15 }17	16 }19	17 }25	20 }22	16 }19
Five or more	9	3	4	2	3	8	2	3
Average	3.14	2.73	2.68	2.73	2.77	2.93	2.77	2.78
Number of mothers (= 100%)	90	195	130	603	234	115	64	1,431

Here is another variable which is U shaped with social class.
The proportion of mothers who reckoned they could afford four or
more children was highest, over a third, for those with husbands in
professional jobs, fell to one in six for the wives of men in skilled
non-manual or manual jobs, then rose to a quarter of those with
husbands in unskilled jobs.   Moreover, there was a significant and
positive correlation between the number of children mothers intended
to have and the number they felt they could afford, $r = 0.54$ $p<0.001$.

Altogether two-thirds intended to have the number they felt they
could afford, a quarter intended to have fewer, one in ten to have
more.   So a sizeable proportion were not intending to have as many
children as they felt they could afford.   This proportion was
rather larger, a third, among those who did not want further children
than among those who did, for which it was a fifth.   Similar
proportions in both groups either had or wanted more.

Among those who wanted further children, the proportion wanting
less than they could afford was highest, 36%, among wives of
professionals; it did not vary significantly among the other social
class groups, for which it was 20%.   There were no social class
differences in the proportion intending to have more than they could
afford.

Among those who did not want further children, the differences
were between middle- and working-class mothers.   Fewer middle-class
mothers had more than they felt they could afford, 3% compared with
11%, more had less than they could afford, 41% against 29%.

So although the wives of professionals reckon they can afford
more children, they are less likely to have or want as many as they
can afford.   Wives of unskilled workers reckon they can afford
rather more children than do other working-class mothers and they
are more likely than middle-class mothers to have more children than
they can afford.

One difficulty for people in deciding whether or not they can
afford another child is that the expense of children is spread over
a long period.   Mothers were asked when they thought children were
more expensive.   ('At what age do you think children are most
expensive - when they are babies, toddlers, starting primary school,
starting secondary school, or later in their teens?')   The majority
thought the main expense was deferred at least until they started
school.   There were clear differences between middle- and working-
class mothers, with more of the middle-class mothers thinking they
were most expensive later on (see Table 91).

TABLE 91 Social class and when children thought to be most expensive

Most expensive when they are:	Middle class	Working class	All mothers
	%	%	%
Babies	8	15	13
Toddlers	6	11	10
Starting primary school	18	25	23
Starting secondary school	28	19	22
Later in their teens	36	24	27
Other answer	4	6	5
Number of mothers (=100%)	421	970	1,458

If the main expense is seen as being in five, ten or fifteen
years' time, expectations about future income may be more important
than present views on its adequacy.

CHANGES IN CIRCUMSTANCES

Two-fifths of the mothers thought they were better off at the time
of interview than they had been eighteen months previously - before
they started their last baby.   A third thought their circumstances
were the same, a quarter that they were now worse off.   ('At the
present time are you better off, about the same, or worse off than
you were eighteen months ago - before you started your last baby?')
There was a clear trend with social class, 58% of those in Social
Class I felt they were better off, and this fell to 39% of those in
Social Class V, while the proportion who thought they were worse off
rose from 16% to 29%.   Mothers who had just had their first baby
were most likely to feel they were worse off, a third of them felt
this compared with a sixth of other mothers.
  The main reason for being worse off was that the mother was no
longer working.   Three-fifths said this, one fifth that they
needed to spend more on the child or children, one in seven mentioned
the increased cost of living.   Two-thirds of those who were better
off said this was because of their husband's job, one in thirteen
because the mother had gone back to work.
  When asked to look ahead five years and say whether they thought
they and their family were likely to be better off, about the same,
or worse off than they were now, the majority of mothers, 62%,
expected to be better off, 30% to be about the same, and only 6% to
be worse off (2% made other comments).   Again more of the middle
class expected to be better off, 78% compared with 55% of the
working class - but within each of these two broad social class
groups there was no clear trend.
  The main reason for expecting to be worse off, given by four-
fifths, was a predicted increase in the cost of living.   Three-
fifths of those expecting to be better off thought their husband
would have a better job or would be earning more, a quarter that
they would be back at work themselves.
  Those who expected to be worse off already had larger families
than the others, an average of 2.37 children compared with 1.91,
but there was no indication that expectations about being better
or worse off in the next five years were related to their intentions
about having further children.   Among those who were hoping for
further children or were uncertain about this, the average number
wanted altogether was similar among those who expected to be the
same, better or worse off, and among those with two children the
proportion wanting a further child was the same for the three groups.
  Once again the results are negative.   Expectations about changes
in their economic situation appear to be unrelated to their
intentions about family size.   But if it has not been possible to
show that economic factors influence the number of children people
have, can it be demonstrated that they affect the time when they
have them?

SAVING AND SPACING

More than one study in North America has suggested that family
income is more strongly related to the timing of demographic events
than to family size (Freedman and Coombs, 1966; Freedman, 1963).
On this study it has already been shown that one in five of the
mothers said they got married when they did for financial reasons.
A similar proportion mentioned housing.   They were also asked
whether there were any things they particularly wanted to do, or
to get or to save up for, before they got married, and if so whether
they had managed to do that.   Just over two-fifths, 43%, said there
was not anything, just under two-fifths, 38%, wanted a home, 'a
place to live', or a deposit for a mortgage, and one-fifth wanted
things for their home.   Typical comments were:
  'Enough money to put down on a house.'
  'A home and some basic pieces of furniture - we already had a
  car.'
  'A house - we tried to save up for a house, but we couldn't -
  sort of inflation then. We could never get the deposit, the
  prices just kept going up and up.'
Three-fifths of those who wanted things had managed to get them,
but two-fifths had not.   They were more likely to have achieved
their ambitions if they wanted things for their home (three-quarters
had got these) than if they had wanted a house or home - only half
of those who wanted that had managed it before they married. Wives
of husbands in skilled manual and skilled non-manual jobs were the
most likely to have wanted to do or get things before they married -
62% of them compared with 52% of the wives of partly and unskilled
workers and fewest of all, 42%, of the wives of professionals. The
nature of their ambitions also varied with social class: three-
quarters of the middle-class against two-thirds of the working-
class mothers who wanted to do something mentioned a house or home.
Even so, the proportion who had done what they hoped had a clear
class gradient from 79% of Social Class I to 48% of Social Class V.
  Mothers who married when they were pregnant were no more or less
likely to say they had wanted to do or get certain things before
they got married, so that having such ambitions did not seem to act
as a deterrent to pre-nuptial conception.   But those who were
pregnant when they married were much less likely to have managed to
get the things they wanted, 27% compared with 72% of other mothers.
  Mothers were also asked whether there were any things they
particularly wanted to do or to get or to save up for before they
had their first baby.   Replies were rather similar, 44% said there
was nothing particular, 28% said a home of their own or a house,
and 26% wanted things for their home.   Among those who were not
pregnant when they married, those who had wanted to do or get
something were less likely to have had a baby within the first two
years of their marriage - 45% of them had done, 67% of those with
no such ambitions.   So here ambitions did seem to lead to a postponement.   But the main difference was in achievement of their
aim.   The proportion who had done this rose from a fifth of those
who had had a baby within eight months of their marriage to a third
of those who had had one between eight and twelve months afterwards,
half of those who had waited between one and two years, three-

quarters with an interval of two to three years, and nine-tenths of
those with a longer interval.   There was no difference with social
class in the proportions who had wanted to do or get things before
they had a baby but the proportion who had achieved their ambitions
fell from 75% of those in Social Class I to 32% in Social Class V.

MOTHER'S WORK

In Chapter 10 it was shown that mothers who had never had a full-
time job had, and wanted, larger families than other mothers, and
that mothers with large families were less likely to be planning to
go back to work.   To what extent, if at all, are their plans for
going back to work related to their attitudes to and experience of
work?   Mothers were asked what they liked about having a job, and
then what they disliked about it.   Replies are shown in Table 92
for mothers already working, those who intended to go back to work
at some stage, and those who did not intend to do so ever.

TABLE 92 Mother's work and views about it

What mother liked about having a job:	Working at time of interview	Planning to go back at some stage	Not planning to go back to work ever	All moth-ers
	%	%	%	%
Money	62	55	46	54
Company, people at work	38	50	48	48
Work itself	32	36	35	35
Independence	16	15	7	14
Personal satisfaction	21	13	10	14
Getting away from home	32	10	7	12
Conditions of work - times, holiday, place	-	1	1	1
Other	-	-	1	-
Nothing	1	4	6	4
What mother disliked about having a job:	%	%	%	%
Conditions of work - times, holiday, place	17	24	21	22
Work itself	15	18	16	17
Too much to do - housework, etc.	9	12	11	11
People at work	2	6	6	5
Problems related to children	13	3	2	4
Too tired, no free time	3	4	5	4
Other	2	3	1	3
Nothing	51	41	48	44
No. of mothers (= 100%)	182	962	240	1,397

The thing they most often mentioned as an advantage was the money.   And this seemed to be related to their intentions about going back to work.   Company and opportunities to meet people was the next most frequently perceived advantage, but this was mentioned less often by those who were already working than by the others. Feelings of independence, personal satisfaction, and the advantages of getting away from home all seemed to be related to getting back to work.   But enjoyment, or positive feelings about the work itself, although mentioned by a third of the mothers was not more common among those already working or those planning to do so. Many mothers gave more than one reason for liking to work.   Typical comments were:

'The money mainly - and getting to know people.   A change from being stuck in the house.'

'The company I suppose.   I loved the job and I didn't want to stop at home all day.   And the money.'

'For me - I got an awful lot of personal satisfaction - and the company - and no time ever to be bored.'

'I liked to have my own money, and meeting people.   The satisfaction of doing a job I really liked.'

Turning to the things they did not like about it, the problem that was mentioned more by mothers who had already gone back to work was making suitable arrangements for the children.

'The fact that you sometimes have to leave a child when you shouldn't - if they have a cold or something.'

The things they most often disliked were related to the times or place of work.

'It was too far to travel - 26 miles a day.'

'I didn't like working Saturday night when everybody was having a good time.'

'The hours were long.   I was working until six at night.'

Those already working mentioned this less often.   So if more work was available near their homes or at convenient times, more mothers might well go back to work earlier.   Once again, views on the work itself were not related to their actions or plans about going back.

An analysis by the social class of the mothers' occupations showed a clear trend in the proportion who said they got personal satisfaction from working from 33% of those in professional or intermediate occupations to 14% in skilled non-manual jobs and 7% in manual occupations.   On the other hand, the proportion who mentioned the company or people at work was highest, 70%, for women doing unskilled manual jobs, 48% for others.   When the social class of the mothers' husbands' occupations were considered rather more of the working- than of the middle-class mothers mentioned the money as an advantage, 57% compared with 49%.

Further evidence that financial considerations played a part in decisions about when to go back to work is that 12% of the mothers who said their income was less than enough for their needs said they would never go back to work compared with 21% of mothers who felt their income was enough or more than enough.   But the proportion already back at work did not differ significantly.

So money may attract mothers back to work, and mothers who intend to go back to work have smaller families than mothers who do not intend to do so.   But mothers' statements about their

intentions may not be fulfilled.   The more factual evidence from
this study relates to mothers already working at the time of interview.   They did not have smaller families than other mothers, and
a relatively high proportion of them were middle class.

UNEMPLOYMENT

Since the experience of the 1930s, with its low birth rates and
high unemployment, there is inevitably much interest in the nature
of the relationship between fertility and unemployment.
    A fifth of the mothers said their husbands had been unemployed
at some time during their marriage and 1.4% that he was unemployed
at the time of interview.   Naturally, the longer the marriage the
more likely he was to have been unemployed - but the differences
were not great.   There was no trend in the proportion unemployed
with the length of marriage if this was less than five years.   It
was 18% for marriages of that duration, 22% for those of between
five and ten years, and 27% for those of ten years or more.   It
is not therefore surprising that the average number of children
they already had increased with the length of time their husbands
had been unemployed - from 1.86 for those who had not been unemployed
at all to 2.88 for those whose husbands had been unemployed for a
year or more.   But the average number of children they intended
to have also increased by 2.51 to 3.25.   And among those with two
children the proportion who wanted additional children increased
from 19% of the mothers whose husbands had never been unemployed
to 48% of those whose husbands had been unemployed for six months
or longer.
    To what extent do these differences reflect differences in
social class and education?   The proportion of mothers whose
husbands had been unemployed at some stage of their marriage
increased from 14% of middle-class mothers to 43% of those in Social
Class V, and the proportion unemployed for a year or more from 1%
to 10%.
    Among the wives of skilled manual and partly skilled workers,
those who had experienced some unemployment had and wanted larger
families than those who had not done so.   The differences in the
other groups are in the same direction but are not significant
(see Table 93).

TABLE 93 Unemployment, social class and family size

Social class	Average present family size		Average intended family size	
	No unem-ployment	Some un-employment	No unem-ployment	Some un-employment
Middle class	1.82(367)	1.94 (54)	2.51(357)	2.60 (52)
Skilled manual	1.83(498)	2.26(109)	2.49(493)	2.79(105)
Partly skilled	2.01(182)	2.78 (65)	2.52(178)	3.20 (65)
Unskilled	1.95 (66)	2.30 (50)	2.68 (66)	2.78 (48)

It was among the middle class and the skilled manual workers that
unemployment seemed to be associated with unintended pregnancy.
The proportion of mothers who said their last pregnancy was
unintended was:

	No unemployment	Some unemployment
Middle class	25% (362)	46% (54)
Skilled manual	33% (493)	47% (107)
Partly skilled	36% (180)	49% (65)
Unskilled	46% (65)	52% (50)

The only differences in their current use of contraception were
related to the sheath and female sterilization.   Among both
skilled manual and partly skilled workers those who had been unemployed were less likely to be using the sheath than those who had
never been unemployed: 14% against 23% in one instance, 12% against
25% in the other.   Among those in Social Classes IV and V the
proportion of mothers who had been sterilized was 13% among those
whose husbands had been unemployed, 2% among the others.
   A factor which contributed to the larger families of those who
had been unemployed was the stage at which the first pregnancy
occurred.   Those who had experience of unemployment were more
likely to have premarital conceptions and to have had their first
baby before they were 20 (see Table 94).

TABLE 94   Unemployment, social class and timing of first pregnancy

	First pregnancy when mother under 20		First baby within 8 months of marriage	
	No unem- ployment	Some un- employment	No unem- ployment	Some un- employment
Middle class	10%(364)	31% (54)	13%(365)	19% (54)
Skilled manual	23%(497)	39%(109)	26%(496)	35%(109)
Partly skilled	24%(181)	39% (62)	25%(181)	33% (64)
Unskilled	47% (66)	58% (50)	32% (66)	58% (50)

One factor contributing to unemployment among men in middle-class
and skilled manual occupations may have been a relative lack of
education in comparison with other men in similar occupations.   The
proportions who had left school as soon as they were old enough to
do so were:

	No unemployment	Some unemployment
Middle class	33% (353)	58% (53)
Skilled manual	83% (491)	93% (107)

To sum up, present data suggest that families who experience some
unemployment want and have rather larger families than those who do
not (see also Freedman and Coombs, 1966).   This seems to be partly
because they start their families at an earlier stage.   But the
implications of these data are limited.   The behaviour of people
who experience unemployment at a time when the unemployment rate is

around 4% does not tell us what will happen to the birth rate in a society with different rates of unemployment.   And it is not necessarily the unemployed whose fertility is most affected by high unemployment.

IN CONCLUSION

It does not appear that mothers who feel their income is enough, or more than enough for their needs, or those who feel better off in relation to other couples they know, or those who expect to be better off in the next five years either have or want more children than mothers who feel more deprived in these respects.   Nevertheless there is a fairly strong, and positive, correlation between feelings about the number of children they can afford and the number of children they intend to have.

Possibly the most illuminating clue that has emerged is that mothers who are married to unskilled workers feel they can afford more children than any other mothers except those married to professional workers.   The evidence seems to point towards groups with different standards, and to that extent to fit in with the findings on social class.   Mothers who are least concerned about material comforts, about secure jobs, about their economic status tend to have relatively large families.

Chapter 13

UPBRINGING AND FAMILY OF ORIGIN

Two factors related to the mother's upbringing are looked at here -
her place of birth and the number of brothers and sisters she had.
In addition, her current contacts and feelings of closeness to her
parents and other relatives are considered.

PLACE OF BIRTH

The great majority of mothers, 86%, were born in England and Wales,
2% in Scotland, 3% in Eire or Northern Ireland, 4% in India or
Pakistan, 2% in Africa or the West Indies, and 3% elsewhere. Clearly
the numbers are too small to do many detailed analyses, but some
basic characteristics are analysed here to try and identify any
major differences and, since some demographic studies exclude
certain foreign-born groups, to see what sort of difference their
inclusion or exclusion is likely to make.
    The average present and intended family size of the groups are
shown in Table 95.

TABLE 95   Family size and place of birth

| | Mother's place of birth | | | | | | All mothers |
	England or Wales	Scotland	Ireland	India or Pakistan	West Indies or Africa	Elsewhere	
Average number of children:							
At time of interview	1.90	2.31	2.04	2.51	2.92	1.92	1.96
Intended	2.52	2.74	2.73	3.28	3.43	2.64	2.58
No.of mothers	1,256	36	47	57	25	51	1,473

Those born in England and Wales had and wanted the smallest families.
Fertility may in general be greater among migrants (see Moser, 1972).
Among the different migrant groups those from India, Pakistan, the
West Indies or Africa had and wanted larger families than those from
Scotland and Ireland. (Differences between India, Pakistan and West
Indies, Africa and between Ireland and Scotland were not significant
and so India, Pakistan, West Indies and Africa were combined, as
were Scotland and Ireland.)

There was no difference between the five main groups of mothers
in the proportion who had their first pregnancy before they were
20, but few of those born in India, Pakistan, Africa or the West
Indies had their first baby when they were 25 or more, 11% compared
with 26% for those born in England and Wales and 30% of the Irish
mothers.

TABLE 96   Place of birth and current use of contraception

	Mother's place of birth					
	Eng-land or Wales	Scot-land	Ire-land	India or Paki-stan	West Indies or Af-rica	Else-where
	%	%	%	%	%	%
Female sterilization	4	11	15	2	12	-
Male sterilization	4	3	2	2	4	-
Pill	44	45	34	26	25	40
Cap	2	3	-	-	4	-
IUD	5	9	6	5	17	4
Sheath	23	11	11	21	17	14
Withdrawal	6	3	6	7	-	10
Safe period	1 }18	3 }18	4 }32	2 }44	- }21	2 }42
Other	2	3	-	2	4	6
None	9	9	22	33	17	24
No. of mothers (= 100%)	1,242	35	47	57	24	50
Proportion in favour of birth control	88%	94%	79%	76%	84%	80%

When asked about their most recent pregnancy, mothers from the
West Indies or Africa were much less likely to say they had intended
to become pregnant that time, only 24% of them compared with 66% of
other mothers.   But it was those born in India or Pakistan, Ireland
and 'elsewhere' who were least likely to be using any method of
contraception around the time of interview.   Those from India or
Pakistan and from Africa or the West Indies were less likely than
those born in England or Wales or Scotland to be taking the pill,
and those from Ireland and from India or Pakistan were more likely

not to be using any method.   A comparatively high proportion of
mothers from Ireland had been sterilized, while a low proportion
from Ireland and Scotland compared with those from England or Wales
were using the sheath.   These differences are shown in Table 96.
   A relatively high proportion of mothers born in the West Indies
or Africa said they had talked to a doctor about birth control, but
the sort of doctors they had seen about this were rather different.
These mothers were less likely than those born in England and Wales
to have discussed birth control with a general practitioner and
more likely to have done so with a doctor at a family planning
clinic or hospital (see Table 97).   They were also more likely to
have discussed it with a health visitor.   In spite, or possibly
because, of these several sources of advice there was some indication
that birth control services were rather less effective or satisfactory for mothers from Africa or the West Indies.   Just over half of
them, 52%, compared with 12% of those born in England and Wales said
that initially they felt sorry their last pregnancy had happened at
all, and the proportion who said they were using some method of
birth control around the time they became pregnant was 40% of those
born in Africa or the West Indies against 21% of those born in
England and Wales.   (This difference might have occurred by chance,
$0.05 < p < 0.10$.)   Although most of them were currently using
effective methods of contraception, the majority of them, 72%
against 42% of other mothers, had only started to use their current
method since their last baby.   It would seem that services only
became effectively available to them after they had a baby, and it
was probably only recently that the services achieved that limited
degree of success.   The numbers are too small for detailed statistical analysis but some idea of the range of the relationships
between these mothers and the services can be seen from these 'case
histories':
(1) Mrs A. had nine children and had used no method of birth control
    until after her last one.   She did not want any more children -
    'I can't even manage the lot I have' and had never discussed the
    number of children she wanted with her husband.   'You can never
    tell how much you will ever have so why do we talk about it?'
    She herself was in favour of birth control but said her husband
    was against it.   'You can't talk to him anything about this at
    all. You just can't talk to him.' But she knew little about
    different methods of birth control and said she would like to
    know more about them all, except the coil.   'I don't know about
    other methods.'   She had talked to her general practitioner and
    a doctor at the hospital but felt her general practitioner did
    not have time to talk about such things as family planning.
    'He has so much people he hasn't got any time to talk about
    anything.'   She'd had her coil fitted six months before the
    interview and had found it very satisfactory, 'I have no trouble
    with it.'
(2) Mrs B. had three children and was uncertain if she wanted any
    more.   'It depends on what the Lord blesses you with.' She was
    not currently using any method of birth control but had used the
    sheath and withdrawal before but only since her last baby, and
    intended to use the sheath again.   'We've got no supplies at the
    moment - must get round to getting some in.' She had been to a

TABLE 97   Place of birth and discussion about methods of birth control

	Mother's place of birth					
	England or Wales	Scotland	Ireland	India or Pakistan	West Indies or Africa	Elsewhere
	%	%	%	%	%	%
General practitioner	66	64	57	56	40	50
Family planning clinic doctor	30	28	21	14	52	36
Doctor at hospital	24	28	38	26	56	24
Doctor at welfare clinic	8	8	11	7	20	8
Private doctor	4	3	2	-	-	6
No discussion with a doctor	16	17	23	28	4	22
Health visitor	26	25	26	25	48	32
Friends or neighbours	62	64	55	42	60	48
Husband	95	92	89	79	92	90
Mother	34	42	28	12	4	12
Father	6	8	2	-	-	4
Other relatives	39	36	45	18	28	38
People having baby at same time	47	53	38	19	48	50
Other non-professionals	2	-	2	2	-	6
No one	3	8	4	16	4	6
No. of mothers (= 100%)	1,253	36	47	57	25	50

family planning clinic and discussed the sheath with the doctor there.

(3) Mrs C. had one child and wanted another.   Since having the baby she had been taking the pill but was worried about her health and the long-term effects.   She felt a coil would be more satisfactory but the 'doctor wouldn't fit it as I wanted another child'. She felt her general practitioner had enough time to talk but 'He is not interested, I can't get on with him.   He always has a long face - you lose your confidence and don't feel like discussing matters with him.'

(4) Mrs D. found her doctor helpful.   'He explained to me about it (coil) not being a 100% so my husband still withdraws to be absolutely safe. He's very patient and understanding.' She had three children and did not want any more.

(5) Mrs E. had been sterilized since her sixth baby which was unintended.   The sterilization had been arranged with the hospital.   She had never discussed birth control with her doctor and did not feel he had enough time to discuss things like that.

(6) Mr and Mrs F., with four children, were using the sheath since the last baby but thought it a rather unsatisfactory method. Mrs F. had decided to be sterilized after the last baby 'but at the last minute my husband changed his mind and wouldn't sign the form'.   She thought a coil would be easier but 'I haven't got time to go to the clinic at the moment as my husband doesn't get back from work until 8.0 p.m. and you have to go around 6.0 p.m.'

Mothers from India or Pakistan had a rather different pattern of experience.   They were the ones least likely to have talked to a doctor or to friends and relatives about birth control.   One obvious reason why those born abroad were less likely to have discussed birth control with their parents is that they were less likely to have seen them recently and to be living near them. The proportion whose parents were living less than a two-hour journey away was 86% for those born in England or Wales, 67% of those born in Scotland, 41% of those born in Ireland, and 19% of the others.

People born in different countries also varied in their social class, religion, and size of family of origin. ('How many brothers and sisters did you have - living with you while you were growing up?')   These variations are shown in Table 98.

The religion (Catholic) of the Irish and (Moslem) of the Pakistanis is likely to contribute to a higher family size, as is also the lower status occupations of those from India and Pakistan. Those born in the West Indies or Africa, India or Pakistan, or Ireland tended to come from large families.   The next section looks at the relationship between the family size of origin and the number of children people had and wanted.

TABLE 98 Place of birth and social class, religion and size of family of origin

	Mother's place of birth					
	England or Wales	Scotland	Ireland	India or Pakistan	West Indies or Africa	Elsewhere
Social class of father's occupation:	%	%	%	%	%	%
I Professional	6	9	5	7	-	14
II Intermediate	15	9	2	9	5	22
III Skilled						
Non-manual	10	15	5	7	-	4
Manual	45	32	65	26	52	37
IV Partly skilled	16	23	14	42	29	23
V Unskilled	8	12	9	9	14	-
Religion:	%	%	%	%	%	%
Catholic	10	11	85	3	16	40
Church of England	73	28	13	5	8	16
Other Protestant	12	52	2	-	48	8
Moslem	-	-	-	37	-	8
Hindu	-	-	-	30	12	-
Other	1	3	-	23	12	16
None	4	6	-	2	4	12
Average number of brothers and sisters	2.58	2.89	4.70	4.57	5.44	3.57
No. of mothers (= 100%)	1,256	36	47	57	25	50

SIZE OF FAMILY OF ORIGIN

The way in which the number of children mothers already had and the number they intended to have varied with their size of family of origin as shown in Table 99. There is a clear trend in both instances. The same trends persisted among women born in England and Wales only.

TABLE 99 Size of family of origin and number of children

	Number of mother's brothers and sisters										
Average no. of children:	0	1	2	3	4	5	6	7	8	9	10+
At time of interview	1.85	1.78	1.91	1.92	2.04	2.17	2.32	2.04	2.53	2.29	2.59
Intended	2.41	2.46	2.54	2.56	2.65	2.72	2.85	2.89	2.98	2.81	3.24
No. of mothers (= 100%)	150	363	303	219	139	112	56	48	32	21	27

Size of family of origin is also related to social class. This
can be seen from the figures below:

Social class of baby's father's occupation	Average size of mother's family of origin
I Professional	1.98 (93)
II Intermediate	2.28 (201)
III Skilled Non-manual	2.13 (131)
III Skilled Manual	2.80 (614)
IV Partly skilled	3.42 (248)
V Unskilled	3.65 (116)

In addition, the proportion who had their first pregnancy before
they were 20 increased with increasing family size of origin (see
also McEwan et al., 1974):

Number of mother's brothers and sisters	Proportion having first pregnancy before they were 20
0	12% (149)
1	17% (360)
2	24% (301)
3 or 4	29% (356)
5 or more	33% (294)

Again the trend was similar if women born outside England or Wales
are excluded.

An attempt to look at the relationship between both social class
and size of family of origin with age at first pregnancy and with
number of children is made in Table 100.

Both social class and size of family of origin still appear to
be related to number of children and age at first pregnancy, but
the strength of the relationship is reduced when the other factor
is held constant.   Mothers from small families (of one or two
children) who are married to men in skilled non-manual jobs have
and want the smallest families, those from large families (of four
or more children) married to men in unskilled or partly skilled jobs
have and want the largest number of children.   With age at first
pregnancy it is the wives of men in professional or intermediate
occupations who come from small families who are least likely to
have a pregnancy in their teens, while those from large families
and married to men in manual jobs are most likely to have that
experience.

Does their size of family of origin influence people's family
size because most appreciated their own experience and wish to
repeat it for their children?   To explore this mothers were asked
whether, looking back now, they would rather have had more brothers
and sisters, fewer brothers and sisters, the number they had or the
same number but different sexes.   Three or four brothers and
sisters, that is a family of four or five children, seemed the most
popular, families with only children the least so (see Table 101).

TABLE 100 Variations in the number of children and age at first pregnancy with size of family of origin and social class

	Number of mother's brothers and sisters				
	0	1	2	3 or 4	5 or more
Social class of father's occupation:	Average no. of children at time of interview				
I or II Professional or Intermediate	1.85	1.75	2.06	1.87	1.81
III Skilled Non-manual	1.46	1.60	2.04	- 1.91 -	
Manual	1.86	1.77	1.83	1.88	2.28
IV or V Partly or unskilled	- 1.95 -		1.95	2.33	2.39
	Average number of children intended				
I or II Professional or Intermediate	2.47	2.51	2.69	2.52	2.66
III Skilled Non-manual	2.22	2.30	2.44	- 2.62 -	
Manual	2.50	2.42	2.52	2.48	2.89
IV or V Partly or unskilled	- 2.43 -		2.51	2.89	2.92
	Proportion having first pregnancy before they were 20				
I or II Professional or Intermediate	6%	7%	8%	16%	19%
III Skilled Non-manual	13%	17%	20%	- 21% -	
Manual	16%	17%	22%	32%	37%
IV or V Partly or unskilled	- 27% -		41%	42%	35%
	No. of mothers on which above figures based				
I or II Professional or Intermediate	34	102	63	69	26
III Skilled Non-manual	24	35	25	33	14
Manual	64	142	130	157	121
IV or V Partly or unskilled	19	73	73	85	114

TABLE 101   Size of family of origin and attitudes towards it

	Number of mother's brothers and sisters							
	0	1	2	3	4	5	6	7 or more
Would rather have had:	%	%	%	%	%	%	%	%
Fewer	-	1	1	5	6	11	16	18
Same number	23	48	82	89	90	85	84	82
More	77	51	17	6	4	4	-	-
No.of mothers (= 100%)	145	363	299	218	138	111	55	125

Those who would have preferred more brothers or sisters tended to have and want larger families themselves, but there was no indication that those who would have preferred fewer planned smaller families themselves. This is suggested by the data in Table 102.

TABLE 102   Views about size of family of origin and number of children

	Number of mother's brothers and sisters				
	0	1	2	3 or 4	5 or more
	Average number of children at time of interview				
Would rather have had:					
Fewer	-	-	-	-	2.16 (44)
Same number	1.59 (34)	1.60(175)	1.82(244)	1.95(319)	2.28(243)
More	1.94(111)	1.95(185)	2.35 (52)	2.21 (19)	-
	Average number of children intended				
Fewer	-	-	-	-	2.84 (44)
Same number	2.22 (32)	2.22(169)	2.44(241)	2.55(316)	2.86(237)
More	2.48(109)	2.67(184)	3.01 (52)	3.44 (17)	-

A simple analysis suggested that those who came from large families were less likely to have seen their mother within the last week, the proportion who had done so declined from four-fifths of only children to three-fifths of those with five or more brothers and sisters. However, if the analysis is confined to those born in England and Wales, this difference disappears. Because of this complication all the analyses in the section on contact with parents are based on mothers born in England and Wales only.

CONTACT WITH PARENTS

Women who had seen their mothers recently had and wanted smaller families than those who had not done so. This is shown in Table 103.

TABLE 103   Contact with mother and family size

	Last saw mother				
Average no. of children:	Lives in same house-hold	Within last 24 hours	Within last week	Within last month	More than a month ago
At time of interview	1.25	1.84	1.89	1.96	2.09
Intended	2.28	2.45	2.52	2.60	2.80
Number of mothers born in England and Wales (= 100%)	44	428	446	143	88

This result might seem unexpected since wives of partly skilled and unskilled workers, who had the largest families, had the most frequent contact with their mothers (see also Willmott and Young, 1960, pp.78-80) (see Table 104).

TABLE 104   Social class and contact with mother

	Social class of baby's father's occupation					
Last saw mother :	I	II	III N	III M	IV	V
	%	%	%	%	%	%
In same household	1	2	2	4	5	4
Seen within last 24 hrs	22 }61	28 }74	33 }79	40 }83	46 }86	44 }85
Seen within last week	38	44	44	39	35	37
Seen within last month	27	14	11	11	10	14
Seen within last year	12	10	6	4	4	-
More than a year ago	-	2	4	2	-	1
Number of mothers born in England and Wales (= 100%)	74	170	105	492	166	92

A possible explanation for mothers who had close contact with their own mothers having and wanting smaller families is, as Table 105 shows, that they were younger.

Among those born in England and Wales the average number of children mothers already had rose from 1.17 for those under 20 to 3.22 for those aged 35 or more, while the number they intended to have rose from 2.29 to 3.17. (The apparent discrepancy of intended family size being smaller than existing number of children arose because the first is confined to children of both the mother and father while the existing number relates to the mother's own children by any man.) When present and intended family size are analysed by both age and contact with mother (Table 106) results suggest that there may still be a tendency, within age groups, for those who had seen their mother within the last twenty-four hours to have smaller families than those who had seen their mothers less recently.

TABLE 105 Age and contact with mother

	Age of baby's mother				
	Under 20	20-24	25-29	30-34	35 or more
Last saw mother:	%	%	%	%	%
In same household	15 ⎫	4 ⎫	2 ⎫	- ⎫	- ⎫
Seen within last 24 hrs	44 ⎬90	38 ⎬81	34 ⎬77	39 ⎬76	33 ⎬71
Seen within last week	31 ⎭	39 ⎭	41 ⎭	37 ⎭	38 ⎭
Seen within last month	5	12	14	15	20
Seen within last year	5	4	8	8	9
More than a year ago	-	3	1	1	-
Number of mothers born in England and Wales (= 100%)	129	441	387	135	55

TABLE 106 Age, contact with mother and family size

	Age of baby's mother			
	Under 20	20-24	25-29	30 or more
Last saw mother:	Average number of children at time of interview			
Seen within last 24 hrs	1.08 (76)	1.51(187)	1.96(138)	2.96 (71)
Seen within last week	⎱1.26 (53)	1.68(173)	1.94(162)	2.66 (70)
Seen more than a week ago	⎰	1.64 (81)	1.86 (87)	3.02 (49)
	Average number of children intended			
Seen within last 24 hrs	2.30 (74)	2.33(182)	2.44(137)	2.82 (70)
Seen within last week	⎱2.27 (53)	2.41(171)	2.52(161)	2.96 (70)
Seen more than a week ago	⎰	2.64 (78)	2.52 (83)	3.06 (48)

The differences are not great but, in view of the association with social class which would suggest trends in the opposite direction, it seems worth exploring further. One possibility is that there is a tendency for women to want to feel part of a family network. If they maintain close contact with their family of origin they may feel less need to have a large family themselves. However, an analysis of mothers who had been born in the same local authority area as their baby compared with mothers born elsewhere in England and Wales showed no significant difference in their present or intended family size. The small differences that were observed were in the opposite direction. (This is not surprising since the proportion of mothers born in the same local authority area as their baby was strongly related to social class increasing from 14% in Social Class I to 49% in Social Class V.) Another possibility is

that women who had close contact with their mothers were more
effective family planners, but there was no indication that they
were using different methods of contraception or that fewer of
their pregnancies were intended - again the observed differences
were in the opposite direction.

Another measure of women's relationships with their family was
a question about who they felt closest to - apart from people in
their own household.   Rather surprisingly, this showed little
variation with age.   Neither were there any clear trends with
social class.

Three-fifths of all the women said they felt closest to one or
other or both of their parents, one-fifth to other relatives, one
in seven to friends or neighbours.   Four per cent said there was
no one outside their household to whom they felt close.   The
relationship between this and their number of children is shown in
Table 107.   Mothers born outside England and Wales and those aged
35 or more have been excluded.

TABLE 107   Number of children and who mother felt closest to

	Average number of children			
	At time of interview		Intended	
Mother	1.78 (535)		2.44 (532)	
Father	1.58 (43)	1.74	2.21 (43)	2.41
Parents	1.63 (134)		2.37 (130)	
Parents-in-law	1.98 (47)		2.77 (45)	
Brother or sister	1.88 (127)	1.91	2.47 (125)	2.60
Other relatives	1.92 (64)		2.74 (64)	
Friends, neighbours or others	1.96 (174)		2.54 (167)	
No one	2.15 (41)		2.92 (39)	

The figures again suggest that the less close mothers' ties are
with their family of origin the more children they have.

DISCUSSION

When people have a fatalistic attitude the concept of wanting or
intending to have children becomes almost irrelevant.   Comparisons
between groups of mothers from different cultures are likely to be
complicated by differing views on their ability to control their
fertility.   Among women who wanted more children fewer of those
born in England and Wales than of those born elsewhere doubted that
they would be able to have the number they wanted, 23% compared
with 34%.   These views may well contribute to the fact that mothers
born outside England and Wales said they intended to have larger
families than native women.   Immigrant mothers already had
larger families and, with the exception of those born in the West
Indies or Africa, they were less likely to be using any method of

birth control.   Their religion is almost certainly one reason for this last observation, and the social class distribution of their occupations may contribute to their desire for larger families, but the numbers are too small to explore these differences in depth.

On size of family of origin it is probably not surprising that mothers from larger families have and want more children than mothers from smaller families even when their social class is taken into account.   Their own experience is likely to influence their expectations and norms, and it has been shown here that most mothers (70%) liked the number of brothers and sisters they had.   It is perhaps more illuminating that the size of their family of origin should be so clearly related to the age at which they have their first pregnancy.   Again they may be following in their mothers' footsteps;   there was no evidence from this study that their sources of help and advice about the care of the baby were related to the number of their siblings.

The findings on family of origin are similar to those on other studies but the observation that women who had seen their mothers recently had and wanted smaller families than those who had not done so is controversial.   The results from this study are in the opposite direction to the hypothesis put forward, but not substan- tiated, in 'Family and Kinship in East London' (Willmott and Young, 1960), that married women who had frequent contacts with their mothers would have relatively large families.   The discrepancy seems unlikely to be explained by the suggestion that the 'traditional' kinship system of support and help had disappeared in the meantime since such a high proportion of the native mothers on the current study had been in touch with their own mothers in the previous week, 80%, which is similar to the proportion of married women in Bethnal Green in 1955 who had done so (ibid., p.30). On this issue it seems inevitable to conclude that further studies are needed.

Chapter 14

HUSBANDS AND MARRIAGE

Up to now most of the analyses have been related to the mothers'
experience and attitudes.   This chapter is concerned with the
fathers' views on family size and contraception, and it also looks
at the relationship between parents and tries to see how the nature
of the marital relationship affects decisions on family size and
the use of birth control.

FATHERS AND CHILDREN

In 'Parents and Family Planning Services' rather more fathers than
mothers hoped they would have more children.   In the present study
there were no significant differences - either overall or taking
those with a particular number of children at the time.   This
suggests that the decrease in the proportion wanting more children
has been even more pronounced among fathers than among mothers.
    When asked how many children they had wanted at the time when
they got married, a higher proportion of fathers than mothers wanted
two and fewer wanted families of four or more, but a higher proportion of mothers than of fathers said they had not wanted any.   This
is shown in Table 108.
    There were no differences between mothers and fathers in their
views on the best number of children for couples more or less like
themselves, but on average fathers reckoned they could afford rather
fewer children than mothers, 2.61 against 2.78.
    When asked about the number of children their husband or wife
wanted, one in ten of both mothers and fathers said there was some
difference between them, but they more often perceived it as the
other member of the couple wanting more than they did - three-fifths
compared with two-fifths who said they wanted more than their
husband or wife.   There was a similar symmetry in their views on
who would get their way over this.   Three-quarters of both the
fathers and mothers who reported some disagreement thought they
personally would get their way.   Some of those who were not going
to get their own way may have suppressed the conflict in their own
minds or they might not have been prepared to talk about it.   Disagreement was rather more often reported by working-class than by
middle-class mothers, 12% against 7%.

TABLE 108   Number of children wanted at time of marriage

	Fathers	Mothers
	%	%
Did not want any	2	5
Uncertain if wanted any	-	1
Wanted:		
One	2	3
One or two	2	2
Two	50	40
Two or three	8	6
Three - or three or four	9	10
Four - or four or five	5	11
Five or more, big family, several	1	3
Some - no idea how many	20	19
Other comment	1	-
Number of parents (= 100%)	262	1,470

As in 'Parents and Family Planning Services', fathers preferred slightly shorter birth intervals than mothers.   The proportion wanting their next baby within 18 months was 19% of fathers, 10% of mothers.   But there were no significant differences in their views on the appropriate interval between marriage and the first child. ('Some people like to start a family straight away when they get married and others to leave it for a while.   How did you feel about this?')

Fathers were asked to recall how they felt when they found their wife was pregnant with the survey baby.   ('Apart from what you feel now - looking back to the time when you found your wife was pregnant - at the time would you rather it had happened a bit earlier or later, or were you pleased she was pregnant then, or sorry it happened at all?')   More of fathers than the mothers recalled being pleased about it, 70% compared with 62%, and they were less likely to have felt 'sorry it happened at all', 6% against 13%.   Similar differences were found in 'Parents and Family Planning Services'.   But unlike that study no difference was found in the present one in the proportion who said they had been using some method of birth control around the time of conception.   This supports the interpretation made last time that the discrepancy was the result of a differential reporting of the use of withdrawal.

ATTITUDES TO BIRTH CONTROL

Fathers were no more or less likely than mothers to say they would like to know more about different methods of birth control, but the methods they were interested in differed slightly.   For instance fathers were less likely to want to know more about female steriliz- ation, 7% compared with 13%.   In addition they were less well informed about the safe period.   Only 42% of fathers compared with 54% of mothers knew when, in a monthly cycle, a woman was most likely to become pregnant.

Fathers' views about the methods of contraception they were
using were similar to the mothers'.   Sterilization and the pill
were viewed as the most reliable, but a third of the fathers thought
there were health hazards associated with the pill, rather more than
half thought the sheath or withdrawal pleasant or easy to use, and
only around a fifth of those using the sheath and a third of those
using withdrawal regarded the method as very satisfactory.

Rather more fathers than mothers, 60% compared with 51%, thought
they might change and use a different method of contraception some
time, and while fewer fathers thought their wives might get an IUD
fitted, 7% against 13%, more thought they might get sterilized
themselves, 19% against 10%.   Both mothers and fathers seemed to
underestimate the willingness of their partners to be sterilized.
This can be seen from Table 109.

TABLE 109   Proportion who would consider sterilization

	Mothers about them- selves	Fathers about their wives	Fathers about them- selves	Mothers about their husbands
	%	%	%	%
Yes	36	23	42	30
Qualified or uncertain	17	22	15	17
No	47	55	43	53
No. of parents not sterilized (= 100%)	1,354	250	252	1,341

It may be that they had never discussed it with their partner or
that people put on a braver front to the interviewers than they did
to their husband or wife.   The greatest difference came from the
interviews with fathers.   From them it would appear that just over
two-fifths would consider being sterilized themselves, but only a
quarter of their wives would consider it.

There was no difference between fathers and mothers in their
reports on the frequency of sexual intercourse in the seven days
before interview: mothers reported an average of 1.86 times,
fathers 1.80.   Gorer reported a similar concordance (1971, pp.114-
15).

HUSBANDS AND WIVES

To try and get some idea of the decision-making process within the
family, mothers and fathers were asked who made most of the big
decisions in their family.   About half of both the mothers and
fathers thought they were made jointly.   For the rest the husband
was more often thought to take the decision than the wife, but this
view was more often held by fathers than by mothers.   A rather
similar picture emerged when they were asked who they thought ought

to be responsible for deciding whether to take precautions to avoid
pregnancy ('Who do you think ought to be responsible for deciding
whether to take precautions to avoid pregnancy - the husband or
wife or both?') except that nine-tenths thought this should be a
joint decision.   Among the others, mothers more often felt it was
up to the wife (see Table 110).

TABLE 110   Marital discussions and decision-making

	Fathers	Mothers
Who makes most of the big decisions in the family:	%	%
Husband	42	33
Wife	6	9
Jointly	49	55
Other comment	3	3
Who ought to be responsible for deciding whether to take precautions to avoid pregnancy:	%	%
Husband	6	4
Wife	3	7
Both	91	89
When first talked about birth control with husband/wife:	%	%
Before marriage	56	48
After marriage before first baby	14	13
Soon after first baby	17	21
Later	7	12
Never	6	6
How easy it is to talk to husband/wife about sex:	%	%
Open and easy	79	77
Not difficult once you get started	14	15
Rather difficult	4	5
Never talked about it	3	3
Has talked to husband/wife about the number of children they want*:	%	%
A lot	40	41
A little	54	49
Not at all	6	10
Number of parents (= 100%)	263	1,473

* Excluding those who had been sterilized.

There was no difference between mothers and fathers in their
descriptions of how easy it was to talk to their partner about sex,
over three-quarters saying it was open and easy but 3% that they
had never done it.   ('Apart from birth control, how easy is it to
talk to your husband/wife about sex? Would you say it was open and
easy, not difficult once you get started, rather difficult, or have
you never talked about it?')

More fathers than mothers said they had talked to their partners about birth control before they were married, and fewer said they had never talked about the number of children they wanted. The differences are in Table 110. These differences suggest that husbands may have either a better memory for discussions with their wives about sex and birth control or that they have a less rigorous or more superficial definition of what constitutes a discussion. Alternatively, men may be less willing to admit to a female interviewer that they had not discussed certain things with their wives.

TABLE 111   Social class and marital discussion and decision-making

	Social class of baby's father's occupation	
	Middle-class	Working-class
Who makes most of the big decisions in the family:	%	%
Husband	33	34
Wife	4	11
Jointly	59	53
Other comment	4	2
Who ought to be responsible for deciding whether to take precautions to avoid pregnancy:	%	%
Husband	2	5
Wife	6	8
Both	92	87
How easy it is to talk to husband about sex:	%	%
Open and easy	83	72
Not difficult once you get started	13	17
Rather difficult	3	6
Never talked about it	1	5
Has talked to husband about the number of children they want*:	%	%
A lot	47	37
A little	49	50
Not at all	4	13
Number of mothers (= 100%)	425	981

* Excluding those who had been sterilized.

Making joint decisions and discussing birth control, sex and the number of children they want may be seen as an index of joint organization in a marital relationship and lack of these as associated with role segregation on the lines described by Bott (1957, p.53). Planning the affairs of the family together is part of her description of a 'joint conjugal role relationship.' But Platt's data throw doubts on the presence of an underlying dimension of jointness/segregation (1969).   The difficulty with the indices in Table 110 is that they are so dependent on verbal communication. Both verbal skills and joint organization are likely to be more common in middle-class families.

The proportion of mothers who said they had discussed birth control with their husbands before their marriage fell from 76% in Social Class I to 22% in Social Class V.   The other differences, shown in Table 111, were also in the expected direction and were between middle- and working-class mothers.   There were no clear trends within the two broad groups.

Although it was expected that decisions would less often be made jointly in working-class families, the difference in the ratio of couples in which the mother perceived herself rather than her husband as making the decisions was more surprising, 1 to 9 of middle-class wives compared with 1 to 3 of working-class ones.

It might be thought that the longer a marriage had lasted the more likely couples would be to have talked about the number of children they want, but it was mothers who had been married for ten years or more who were most likely to say they had never discussed this with their husbands, 27% compared with 8% of mothers who had been married for less long.   Part, but not all, of this difference apparently arose because older women were less likely to have discussed it.   The proportion who said they had done so declined from 94% of those under 20 to 77% of those aged 35 or more.

The proportion of mothers who said they had not talked about the number of children they wanted with their husband at all rose from 6% of those with one child to 48% of those with five or more.   Those who had not discussed it at all were less likely to be using the sheath, 16% compared with 24%, and more likely not to be using anything at all, 22% against 10%, than those who had done so.   Their last pregnancy was less likely to have been intended, 57% against 70%.   This ties up with Rainwater's finding that 'couples in less segregated relationships are...more likely to use an effective method (of contraception)' (1965, p.293).

These associations between family size, unintended pregnancy and use of contraception with discussion about the number of children they wanted existed mainly in working-class rather than middle-class couples.   This seemed to be because the main differences were between those who had not talked about it at all and the others, and so few, 4%, of the middle class had not done so.   Among the working class the proportion who had not discussed it with their husbands rose from 7% of those with one child to 59% of those with five or more;   the proportion currently using a sheath was 23% among those who had discussed it, 15% among those who had not, while the proportions using nothing at all in the two groups were 11% and 22%;   and the proportions whose last pregnancy was intended were 67% and 56%. Among the middle class the only significant difference was in the proportion of intended pregnancies, 82% among those who had discussed it a lot, 69% among those who had talked about it a little or not at all.

The proportion of mothers who had conceived their first baby before they were married did not vary with mothers' reports on their discussions of the number of children they wanted, nor was it related to who made the big decisions.   But, not surprisingly, the proportion of premarital conceptions was lower, 12%, if mothers said they had discussed birth control with their husband before their marriage, than if they had not done so, 36%.   It also varied with their views on who ought to be responsible for deciding whether to take precautions to avoid pregnancy.   It was only 6% for those who thought it should be the husband, 25% for the others.   This striking difference was probably related to the methods of birth control used (see Table 112).   It did not seem to result from mothers who had had an unintended pregnancy being less inclined to feel it should be their husbands' responsibility, since mothers' statements about whether or not their last pregnancy was intended did not vary with whom they thought should be responsible for deciding whether to take precautions to avoid pregnancy.

TABLE 112   Current use of contraception and who mothers felt should be responsible for deciding whether to take precautions to prevent pregnancy

	Who ought to take responsibility		
	Husband	Wife	Both
	%	%	%
Female sterilization	9	5	4
Male sterilization	4	2	3
Pill	17	51	44
Cap	-	1	2
IUD	4	13	5
Sheath	41	9	22
Withdrawal	8	1	7
Safe period	-	3	1
Others	2	2	2
None	15	13	10
No. of mothers (= 100%)	53	108	1,285

The sheath was much more likely to be used if the mother felt this decision should be the husband's, while the pill and IUD were more often used if she thought it should be the wife's.   The strong association between premarital conceptions and who the mothers felt should take this responsibility may well arise because methods which do not involve medical consultation are more acceptable to unmarried couples and more effective because they do not demand much planning ahead.

Unintended pregnancies were less common among those who had discussed birth control with their husbands before they were married and most frequent among those who had not done so until some time after their first baby.   This is shown in Table 113.   They were also slightly less frequent among those who felt most of the big decisions were made jointly rather than by either the husband or wife, 32% compared with 39%.   There was a clear trend in the proportion who said their last pregnancy was intended with whether they had discussed the number of children they wanted a lot, a little or not at all.

TABLE 113   Unintended pregnancies and marital relationships

	Proportion whose last pregnancy was intended	Number of mothers (= 100%)
When first talked about birth control with husband:		
Before marriage	77%	700
After marriage, before first baby	62%	183
Soon after first baby	56%	308
Later	38%	173
Never	59%	79
Has talked to husband about the number of children they want:		
A lot	73%	543
A little	67%	659
Not at all	57%	129

TABLE 114   Frequency of intercourse and discussion of sex and birth control

	Average reported frequency of intercourse in week before interview	Number of mothers on which averages based	Proportion not answering question on frequency of intercourse
When first talked about birth control with husband:			
Before marriage	1.96	673	5%
After marriage, before first baby	1.91	177	3%
Soon after first baby	1.93	297	4%
Later	1.65	158	10%
Never	1.00	71	12%
How easy it is to talk to husband about sex:			
Open and easy	1.99	1064	4%
Not difficult once you get started	1.60	209	6%
Rather difficult	1.23	66	6%
Never talked about it	0.92	36	23%

Mothers who found it difficult to discuss sex with their husbands
and those who had never talked to their husbands about birth control
reported a lower frequency of intercourse than other mothers. This
is shown in Table 114.

The low rate of reported intercourse among those who had never
talked about sex or birth control might have arisen because mothers
who were shy of discussing these subjects with their husbands were
shy of telling interviewers about their sexual activities. Certainly
the proportion who did not answer this question were relatively high
in these groups.   But it may be that those who do not enjoy sex are
less willing to talk about it and also have it less frequently.   Age
differences in the groups, discussed in the next section were not
large enough to account for the variations in Table 114.

AGE AND MARITAL RELATIONSHIPS

Older mothers were the ones least likely to have discussed birth
control with their husbands.   The proportion who had not done so
was 3% among those under 30, 12% for those aged 30-34, and 19% for
those aged 35 or more.   But of course only mothers who had a young
baby are included in the sample, and among older mothers there was
a high proportion with unintended pregnancies, while among younger
ones there was a high proportion of premarital conceptions. These
two factors probably explain why most of the variations in marital
relationships with age are U, or rather inverse U, shaped.   The
proportion who had discussed birth control before their marriage,
the proportion who said discussion of sex was open and easy, the
proportion who thought they should both be responsible for deciding
whether to take precautions to avoid pregnancy, and the proportion
who said that most of the big decisions in their family were made
jointly, were all highest among those aged 25-29.   This is shown
in Table 115.

Older mothers aged 35 or more were more likely than others to
say that their husbands should take responsibility for decisions
on whether to use birth control.   But in general the findings here
do not indicate a movement towards more joint decision-making and
more open and easy discussion of sex and birth control.

When the difference in the ages of the husband and wife was
considered, it seemed that couples were less likely to discuss birth
control before marriage if the wife was much younger than the
husband.   The proportions who had done so were 58% when the wife
was older than the husband, 52% when they were the same age (within
twelve months), 48% if the wife was one to four years younger, and
44% if she was five or more years younger.

TABLE 115 Age and marital relationships

	Mother's age				
	Under 20	20-24	25-29	30-34	35 or more
When first talked about birth control with husband:	%	%	%	%	%
Before marriage	34	49	58	40	36
After marriage before first baby	21	14	11	9	9
Soon after first baby	37	25	17	14	14
Later	6	8	11	25	22
Never	2	4	3	12	19
How easy it is to talk to husband about sex:	%	%	%	%	%
Open and easy	76	77	82	67	65
Not difficult once you get started	20	15	12	20	20
Rather difficult	3	5	4	7	7
Never talked about it	1	3	2	6	8
Who the mother thought ought to be responsible for taking decisions about whether to prevent pregnancy:	%	%	%	%	%
Husband	2	2	3	7	11
Wife	12	8	7	4	8
Both	86	89	90	88	81
Other comment	–	1	–	1	–
Who makes most of the big decisions in the family:	%	%	%	%	%
Husband	44	37	31	34	39
Wife	11	9	8	12	7
Both	44	53	60	53	54
Other comment	1	1	1	1	–
Number of mothers (= 100%)	146	544	484	201	87

LOOKING AFTER THE BABY AND DOING THE HOUSEWORK

The division of tasks within the family and the extent to which the father is involved in housework and looking after the children, is a facet of a marital relationship that Bott's study suggests is likely to be related to their pattern of decision-making. She found that 'Couples who stressed the importance of joint decisions also had many shared and interchangeable tasks in housework and child care' (1957, p.54).

Mothers were asked who had helped them most in looking after the baby and fathers who had helped their wives most. Half, 49%, of the mothers said their husbands had helped most; rather more, 58%,

of the fathers said they had done so.   Similar proportions of
each, 14%, said the mother's mother had been most helpful, rather
more of the mothers, 24%, than of the fathers, 18%, said no one
had helped.

If mothers said it was their husbands who had helped them with
the baby most they were more likely to have discussed birth control
before they were married, 53% against 44%, to say most of the big
decisions in their family were made jointly, 59% against 51%, that
discussion of sex with their husband was open and easy, 80% against
73%, and they were less likely to say they had never discussed sex,
2% against 4%, or birth control, 4% against 7%.   So the extent to
which the husbands helped with the baby was related to the mothers'
perceptions about decision-making in the family and their discussion
of certain issues.

The different things fathers had done for the baby are shown in
Table 116.

TABLE 116 Mothers' and fathers' reports of what the fathers had
done for the babies

	Mothers	Fathers
	%	%
Changed his/her nappy	74	77
Got up to him/her at night	69	82
Fed him/her	89	95
Bathed him/her	28	32
Dressed him/her	53	66
Looked after him/her while mother has been out for an hour or more	91	92
Taken him/her out	53	56
None of these	2	1
Number of parents (= 100%)	1,432	261

Fathers reported doing rather more things than the mothers said
they did.   But the differences in changing the baby's nappy,
bathing him, taking him out and looking after him while the mother
was out might have occurred by chance.

Not surprisingly, the father was rather more likely to have done
things for the baby if the mother said he was the person who had
helped most.   For example, when the mother said this, 85% also
said he had changed the baby's nappy compared with 63% who did not
feel he had been the most helpful.   In view of this association it
is rather surprising that there were no significant variations
between working- and middle-class mothers in the proportions saying
their husbands had done different things for the baby, as more of
the middle- than of the working-class mothers said their husbands
had been the person who helped them most, 55% compared with 45%.
There was no difference between middle- and working-class mothers
in the proportion who said no one had helped them with the baby,
but more working-class women said their own mothers had given the
most help, 16% compared with 10% of middle-class women.   The lack

of class differences in the help that fathers gave with the baby
persisted even when an attempt was made to take the number of times
he did the various things into account.   It contrasts with a clear
difference in the other household tasks he undertook.   Three-
quarters of the middle-class mothers compared with three-fifths of
working-class ones said their husbands had helped with the washing-
up in the previous seven days.   And a score based on the number of
times in the previous seven days that he had helped with the washing-
up, making the beds, cooking and looking after the children averaged
8.13 for middle-class, 6.94 for working-class husbands.

It might be thought that men who often took part in such household tasks as washing-up might be the ones who were prepared to take
over the practical responsibility for contraception, and the household task score was in fact relatively high, 7.97, for those using
the sheath, and it was comparatively low, 6.86, for those using no
method around the time of interview.

But the basic question here is whether women whose husbands
helped with the housework and looking after the children had or
wanted different sized families from those whose husbands did not
play this role.   The evidence suggests that in families with four
or more children the husband took a less active part in these tasks.
For instance, the proportion who had helped with the washing-up was
64% if there were less than four children in the family, 50% if
there were four or more.   And the mother said it was her husband
who helped her most with the baby in 50% of the families with less
than four children and 34% for larger ones.   There did not appear
to be any significant trends among those with one, two or three
children.   There were no clear differences in their family size
intentions, or in the proportion who wanted further children when
their present family size was held constant.   The differences in
achieved family size seemed to result from differential achievement
of intentions: the proportion of mothers who said their last
pregnancy was intended was 70% when the husband had helped with the
baby most, 59% when he had not done so.

Co-operation in one sphere was apparently related to co-operation
in others.

RELATIONSHIPS WITH KIN

Was there any evidence that relationships with family of origin were
related to the nature of their marital relationship and discussions
of birth control and family size?   Those who felt closest to their
parents were more likely to have discussed birth control with their
prospective husband before they were married than those who felt
closest to other relatives or friends or neighbours, 52% compared
with 44%, while those who did not feel close to anyone outside their
own household were the least likely to have done so, 30%.   These
findings suggest that a mother's relationship with her family of
origin and her relationship with her husband are often complementary
and supportive rather than competitive.   Those who make satisfactory
relationships in one sphere are probably more likely to have satisfactory relationships in another.   In the previous chapter, it was
shown that those who said they did not feel close to anyone outside

their own household had the largest families.   They also seemed to
have a more segregated role-relationship with their husband;   not
only were they less likely to have discussed birth control with him
before their marriage, they were less likely to have found discussion
of sex with him open and easy, 65% compared with 77%, and more
likely not to have talked about it at all, 11% compared with 3%, and
fewer of them thought that husband and wife ought to decide together
about taking precautions to avoid pregnancy, 74% compared with 89%.
In addition a higher proportion of their last pregnancies were
unintended, 49% compared with 35%, and they were less likely to have
discussed the number of children they wanted with their husbands,
22% of them said they had not done so at all, 9% of other mothers.
These findings do not support the hypothesis that in the absence of
social relationships outside the family married couples will have a
more joint relationship (see Harris, 1969, p.174).   They add
further weight to the need for a reappraisal of the original Bott
hypothesis (Turner, 1967).

Frequency of contact with parents did not seem to be clearly
related to the various measures of the marital relationship used on
this study.

SUMMING UP

This study supports the findings from other inquiries that husbands
and wives who discuss their problems and decisions have smaller
families than those who do not.   They also share more of the household tasks and care of children.   One reason for their smaller
families appears to be that they are more effective in their use
of contraception.

But the findings on pre-marital conception suggest that the
couple may be more successful in avoiding an unintended pregnancy
before marriage if the male partner takes responsibility for contraception.

Chapter 15

SOME CONCLUSIONS AND SPECULATIONS

In this final chapter I do three things: discuss the main findings
of the study, emphasizing the results which are new and those that
are controversial; then, in relation to birth control services, I
consider some of the possible dangers of recent developments; and
finally speculate about the implications of these findings for the
future. The results are discussed under four broad headings -
intentions, economic influences, family relationships and birth
control.

INTENTIONS

For many couples intentions about family size are neither firm nor
static. As many as 10% of the mothers were uncertain whether or
not they wanted another baby, and another 15% said that they did
not want another but that they might change their mind about this
later. If a quarter express such doubts after they have had at
least one child, the number of children people say they want at the
time of their marriage is unlikely to be a very accurate prediction
of the number they, as individuals, will eventually want or have,
although for groups of mothers changes in intentions seemed equally
balanced in the two directions, towards larger and smaller family
sizes.

In terms of changes in time between 1967/68 and 1973 two clear
trends emerged. In 1973 parents were intending to have smaller
families than they were in 1967/68. This held both at the time of
interview and for their reported feelings at the time of their
marriage. The main differences in their views at the time of
interview were among those who had two or three children at the
time. Among those with two the proportion who said they wanted
more dropped from 32% in 1967/68 to 20% in 1973, and among those
with three this proportion fell even more steeply from 20% to 11%.
The trend is to less variation in family size since there is no
indication that single-child families are becoming more popular.
And the proportion of mothers who already had four or more children
had fallen from 14% in 1967/68 to 9% in 1973 - although among these
mothers, the proportion who wanted more children had not declined

significantly.   The stereotype of the two- or three-child family
is becoming more and more common.   One of the distinguishing
characteristics between this demographically important division of
those who want two and those who want three is the sex distribution
of the first two.   Seventeen per cent of those who had a boy and
a girl wanted another child, compared with 26% of those who had two
of the same sex.   But for larger families the desire for a mixed-
sex family seemed a less important criterion in 1973 than in 1967/
68.

Apart from the desire for smaller families, the other main change
between 1967/68 and 1973 in relation to intentions was an apparent
increase in uncertainty.   The proportion who said that they had
been uncertain when they married about whether they wanted any
children or about the number they wanted rose from 11% of mothers
in 1967/68 to 20% in 1973.   And among those with two children, the
proportion who were uncertain whether or not they wanted another
rose from 10% to 15%.   It may seem plausible to attribute this to
an increase in uncertainty about their economic situation, but the
data suggest that the effect is not a simple one.

ECONOMIC INFLUENCES

Economic theories have not been notably successful in interpreting
variations in fertility, but economic considerations were the
reasons most commonly given by mothers for not wanting further
children or for choosing a particular family size.   In a recent
paper (1975), Leibenstein suggests
    that populations are divided into social status groups that have
    different tastes, who may to some degree have different desires
    for children (but not simply because of an income difference),
    and who especially see the whole cost of their expenditures,
    including expenditures for children, from the viewpoint of vastly
    different preference structures.
Sociologists may feel such a statement is naive.   They are unlikely
to challenge the premise that social status groups react differently
to economic questions, but they are more likely to query whether
models of economic preference structures are relevant for any groups.

The data from this study might, at first sight, suggest that
while economic theories do not hold for the working classes, that is
people in manual occupations, they may work for middle-class people
in non-manual jobs.   Among the middle class the number of children
they had, wanted and estimated they could afford was highest in
Social Class I, the professionals, and lowest among those in skilled
non-manual jobs.   In contrast, among the working class, both
achieved and wanted family size were lowest in the group that was
most well-off, the skilled.

The trends among the middle class might appear to tie up with
social class variations in housing and in people's view about their
income and economic situation, since those in Social Class I were,
if anything, less likely than those in Social Class III non-manual
to regard their income as inadequate for their needs, and less
likely to feel they were worse off than other families they knew
well.   However, even when the middle class were taken on their own,

feelings of relative affluence were not associated with either having or wanting larger families.   The only measure of parents' views on their economic situation which correlated in a positive way with their present and intended family size was their opinion about the largest number of children they reckoned they could afford to bring up reasonably.   This obviously subjective question related to family size both overall and for middle- and working-class mothers separately.   Moreover it had a U-shaped distribution in relation to social class.   But, as with the number of children people had and wanted, the number of children they felt they could afford was not greater among those who felt they were better off than other families they knew well or among those who thought their income was more than enough for their needs.

So although many people perceive money as a major factor in their decisions about their family size, the data from this study have not shown the way in which its influence operates.   The process may be rather more subtle and complicated, it may work through other channels than the ones explored here, or people may be rationalizing or giving what they feel is an acceptable answer.   A further indication that economic criteria do not play a simple and large part in accounting for differences in family size is that few mothers felt their family size intentions would be influenced if their household income went up by £5 a week, that is by 10% on average (Central Statistical Office, 1974, p.115).

Since family size intentions in 1973 varied so little (78% of mothers either wanted two or three children or already had two or three and did not want any more) it is not surprising that few clear-cut factors relating to them emerged.   Economic influences and uncertainty may play a greater part in affecting the general level of these intentions.   These more general influences, affecting groups rather than individuals within a group, seem more likely to operate on the middle range of families, with those at the two extremes being rather less affected.   At one end money and influence may enable families to ignore norms, at the other end, lack of money and influence may mean families do not share the same norms (Askham, 1975).

FAMILY RELATIONSHIPS

One part of the study findings supports the results from other inquiries - that husbands and wives who discuss their problems and decisions have smaller families than those who do not.   Part of the explanation seems to lie in their more effective use of contraception.

Another finding is in conflict with the implications, if not the findings, from other studies.   This is the observation that women who see their mothers relatively frequently have and want comparatively small families.   One possible explanation is that those who have little or no contact with their parents may want to compensate for this by having more children than those who retain ties with their family of origin.   Another possibility, with some data to support it, is that a mother's relationship with her parents and her relationship with her husband are often complementary and

supportive rather than competitive.   It seems plausible that
people who make satisfactory relationships with their parents are
also more likely to make a satisfactory relationship within their
marriage, they are then more likely to discuss their views and
problems openly with their husbands and this is associated with
smaller families.

The argument derived from other studies (Bott, 1957; Harris, 1969;
Turner, 1967; Willmott and Young, 1960) is that women who are close
to their mothers have a less close relationship with their husband,
the husband and wife have more segregated roles and larger families,
possibly because they rely to a greater extent on more traditional
and less efficient methods of birth control.   The theory on which
this argument is based is quite elaborate and sophisticated.   But
there seems little or no statistical data to support it.

BIRTH CONTROL

There have been many developments in the techniques of birth control
in the last ten years, but there also has been a revolution in the
availability of different methods.   Safe and legal abortion is
accessible to wider groups and there have been significant changes
in attitudes to the acceptability of abortion among women and among
doctors.   The proportion of mothers who thought a woman with
several children ought to be able to get an abortion if she wanted
one doubled, from one-third to two-thirds, between 1967/68 and 1973.
In these five years the proportion of mothers depending on the two
most effective methods of birth control, sterilization and the pill,
more than doubled.   Doctors have become a more frequent source of
advice and help, and by 1973 over half the mothers were using a
method of contraception which could only be obtained through
doctors.   The dissemination of information and advice about medical
methods of contraception has become more widespread.

DANGERS OF CURRENT DEVELOPMENTS IN BIRTH CONTROL SERVICES AND
INFORMATION

One aspect of these developments seems to me a major cause for
concern - I would suggest that the medical appropriation (Illich,
1975) of contraception presents dangers and difficulties.   This
seems a particular problem for young people at the time of their
first experiences of sex.   Knowledge of the pill is widespread,
access to it is restricted to medical channels.   Yet if the
advantages and simplicity of the pill are generally well known,
people may be less ready to accept the disadvantages of non-medical
methods which may be less reliable but are more immediately
available.   There may be some danger that the propaganda against
such methods as withdrawal and the safe period (see the comics by
Smith, 1973, 1975) will be successful in discouraging people from
using these methods but will not be successful in encouraging them
to use other, more effective methods.   The net result will be an
increase in unprotected intercourse.

It may be more realistic to accept that many people will not be so calculating and so open about their initial sexual experiences that they wait until they have the protection of a medical method. It may be preferable to inform them about non-medical methods, and, shifting the argument a stage further, about methods which do not involve an appliance.   If young people are taught about the stage in a monthly cycle when women are most likely to conceive they may be prepared to confine their earlier experiences to a time when the likelihood of conception is not maximized, while at the same time recognizing that the possibility of conception still exists.

For mothers who have already had a child the medical appropriation of birth control may have undermined the traditional methods they have used in the past.   As well as making them more aware of the unreliability of such methods they may also be more aware of other disadvantages - a restriction of the times when they can have intercourse or the imposition of a regime requiring self control.   The sad fact is that for many people there is no reliable method of contraception which is reversible, free from health hazards and pleasant and easy to use.   The choice of contraception is a compromise involving the acceptance of at least one disadvantage. Sterilization is not reversible, the pill is seen as involving unknown long-term risks as well as immediate side effects for some people, the coil is often quite difficult to obtain, involves fitting which is perceived as unpleasant and may give rise to side effects with the added problem that it is not certain how it works; other methods interfere with the pleasures of intercourse and some are unreliable.

Although the use of reliable methods may have increased dramatically, it is less certain whether couples will be prepared to continue using the pill for many years, or how many will find the IUD acceptable over a long period.   Because of the pill people may have higher levels of expectation for their contraception than they had previously.   They want and expect contraceptives to be reliable, they do not want them to interfere with intercourse.   At the moment these expectations are unrealistic unless they are prepared to accept possible health hazards or permanent sterility.   Doctors have appropriated a role, but need better techniques to carry it out.

There is the additional problem that if doctors appropriate the role of decision-makers and decide that men or women should not be sterilized before a certain age or before they have had a certain number of children, then sterilization will be inaccessible to the vast number of people who have and want a small family at an early stage of their marriage.   They may become eligible in the doctors' terms later on, but it may need a birth or abortion to act as a catalyst for such a decision and process.

In a number of ways this study has concentrated on people who may be given more help and advice on birth control than other groups. In the process of having a baby mothers come into contact with many people who may give help and advice about birth control.   In addition, by having a baby, a couple have drawn attention to their fertility.   Both they themselves and the professionals they come into contact with are likely to realize that action is needed if a further pregnancy is to be avoided or postponed.   The needs of young people and others who have not had any children and of older people who completed their desired family some time ago are not highlighted in the same way - except by abortion.

IMPLICATIONS FOR THE FUTURE

Between 1967/68 and 1973 parents' family size intentions decreased.
This may have been partly because more parents in 1973 felt able to
control the number of children they had.   There is no evidence
that one-child families are increasing in popularity so it seems
unlikely that intentions will decline much further since the great
majority of parents now want two or three children.   If they could
control the sex of their children a higher proportion would possibly
opt for two rather than three children but initially, an ability to
determine sex might lead to a sizeable spurt in the birth rate:
more of those who already had two or three children of the same sex
might decide to have another if they could be sure of then having a
mixed-sex family.

Other factors which this study suggests may encourage the trend
to slightly smaller wanted families are a further increase in the
proportion of home owners or buyers, an increase in the proportion
of women having some further education, an increase in joint
decision-making within a family, and a decrease in the proportion
of women not working at all before they marry or start a family.

The main factor which seems likely to lead to an increase in
intended family size is any further increase in the proportion
marrying at an early age.

Turning now to the achievement of, or failure to achieve,
intentions.   The trend to more effective use of contraception among
married couples may well continue but cannot be assumed.   Anxieties
about the pill may discourage its prolonged use by many mothers,
and when the pill is rejected professional services are not always
sought, and even when they are they may not be helpful about
alternatives.

But the greatest potential, in demographic terms, for reducing
unintended pregnancies is probably among the young.   A quarter of
the mothers were pregnant when they married, and this proportion
was two-fifths for those married before they were 20.   Less than
a third of those pregnant at the time of their marriage said they
had intended to become pregnant then, but only a quarter said they
were using some method of contraception around the time they became
pregnant.   I would doubt if these numbers are likely to fall
greatly if services and education continue along present lines.   If
the abortion law is amended, along the lines of the Abortion (Amendment) Bill, they will almost certainly increase.   One way in which
they might be reduced is by making the pill more accessible, through
pharmacists without a doctor's prescription.

As time goes on people may have higher expectations not only
about suitable methods of contraception but also in relation to
achieving their intentions and not having more children than they
intended.   Although in 1973 couples were using more effective
methods of contraception and fewer had conceived accidentally while
they were using some method than five years previously, they was no
parallel decrease in the proportion of pregnancies that were
initially unwanted.   Expectations had increased so that they kept
pace with the increase in contraceptive efficiency in the same sort
of way that they seem to increase with higher material standards of
living.   If the proportion of unintended pregnancies was reduced

the main effect would probably be on the spacing of births rather
than on final family size.   It would also probably reduce slightly,
but would certainly not eliminate, social class variations in
family size.

THE SAMPLE

THE STUDY AREAS

The 25 study areas were selected by using the topographical arrangement of registration divisions which lists the districts and local
authority areas by region and County (General Register Office, 1972,
p.212).   The total number of births in 1970 was divided by 25 to
determine the sampling interval and a number under this was chosen
at random to give a starting point.   Births in the Counties in
1970 were summed cumulatively so that each County was allocated a
series of numbers corresponding to the number of births in the
County in 1970 (Office of Population Censuses and Surveys, 1972a).
When the Counties in which the sampling points fell had been
identified, local authority areas within the Counties were listed
in order of the topographical arrangement but grouped together so
that there were at least 350 births in 1970 in any unit.   When a
local authority area was divided between two or more registration
districts, it was generally taken in the order in which it first
appeared in the list and subsequent entries were ignored. Numbers
were allocated to the various areas in the Counties again in
relation to the number of births in the areas in 1970.   The areas
in which the sampling points fell became the study areas.   They are
listed in Table A.

THE SAMPLE OF BIRTHS

Eighty legitimate births (multiple births were treated as a single
birth as the sample unit was the mother or father not the babies)
registered during the last quarter of 1972 were selected at random
by the Office of Population Censuses and Surveys for each of the
25 study areas.   Within each area 67 of the 80 were then allocated,
again at random, to the sample of mothers, the other 13 to the
sample of fathers.
     A number of comparisons can be made to see whether the sample was
representative.   These fall into three groups:
 1 The initial sample selected can be compared with data about all
    legitimate births in England and Wales for data that are recorded

TABLE A   The study areas

Areas	Number of births in 1970		Proportion of births in rural districts
1 Maryport and Workington (Cumberland)			
Maryport U.D.	186 }	637	-
Workington M.B.	451		
2 Northumberland North First			
Belford R.D.	56 }		
Berwick-upon-Tweed M.B.	240	403	40%
Norham and Islandshires R.D.	41		
Glendale R.D.	66		
3 Kingston-upon-Hull C.B. (Yorkshire E. Riding)		5,048	-
4 Sheffield C.B. (Yorkshire W. Riding)		8,214	-
5 Tadcaster R.D. (Yorkshire W. Riding)		556	100%
6 Buxton (Derbyshire)			
Buxton M.B.	292 }		
Whaley Bridge U.D.	58	529	-
New Mills U.D.	179		
7 Oldham C.B. (Lancashire)		1,954	-
8 Horwich (Lancashire)			
Horwich U.D.	273 }		
Westhoughton U.D.	253	614	-
Blackrod U.D.	88		
9 Clowne (Derbyshire)			
Clowne R.D.	313 }		
Staveley U.D.	278	744	42%
Bolsover U.D.	153		
10 Wellingborough R.D. (Northamptonshire)		378	100%
11 Stoke-on-Trent C.B. (Staffordshire)		4,146	-
12 Birmingham C.B. (Warwickshire)		18,141	-
13 Royal Leamington Spa M.B. (Warwickshire)		831	-
14 East Dereham (Norfolk)			
East Dereham U.D.	140 }	402	65%
Mitford and Launditch R.D.	262		
15 Slough M.B. (Buckinghamshire)		1,613	-

Table continues

TABLE A   The study areas (continued)

Areas		Number of births in 1970	Proportion of births in rural districts
16 Barking L.B.	(Greater London)	2,202	-
17 Enfield L.B.		3,834	-
18 Islington L.B.		3,867	-
19 Southwark L.B.		4,050	-
20 Andover M.B. (Hampshire)		508	-
21 Rochester M.B. (Kent)		1,056	-
22 Walton and Weybridge U.D. (Surrey)		746	-
23 Plymouth C.B. (Devon)		4,093	-
24 Bath C.B. (Somerset)		1,070	-
25 Llantrisant and Llantwit Fardre R.D. (Glamorgan)		747	100%

on the non-confidential part of the birth certificate and which are analysed nationally.

2   The sample for which interviews were obtained can be compared with those for which there was no interview for data on the non-confidential part of the birth certificate.

3   The sample for which interviews were obtained can be compared with data about all legitimate births in England and Wales.

For a number of factors more than one type of comparison can be made so it is simpler to make the different types of comparisons together under headings for the various factors.

Urban and rural areas

Eighteen per cent of the births in the initial sample were in rural districts compared with 22% of all births in England and Wales in 1972. (National figures for births are taken from Office of Population Censuses and Surveys, 1974a.)   Success rates did not differ significantly between urban and rural areas.

Baby's sex

In the initial sample 51.1% of the babies were male compared with 51.5% among legitimate births in 1972 - a difference which might well have occurred by chance as might the slight difference in the proportion of successful interviews - 88% for boys, 86% for girls.

Birth place of parents

The birth-place of parents is only published nationally for all
births both legitimate and illegitimate. Comparisons in Table B
show that births to Indian and Pakistani mothers and fathers seem
to be somewhat over-represented in the sample.   Births to West
Indian mothers, on the other hand, are slightly under-represented,
possibly because the national figures include illegitimate births.
    Response rates were highest for parents born in the UK.   They
were also relatively high for those born in India and Pakistan,
but lowest for those born in the Irish Republic.

TABLE B   Birth place of parents

	Mothers			Fathers		
	England and Wales 1972	Initial sample	Proportion of successes	England and Wales 1972	Initial sample	Proportion of successes
	%	%		%	%	
United Kingdom	88.6	87.9	88%	88.0	87.3	88%
Irish Republic	2.6	2.7	77%	2.6	2.7	74%
India, Pakistan and Bangladesh	2.9	4.0	83%	3.3	4.2	82%
Africa	0.7	0.8		0.8	0.9	
West Indies	1.5	1.0	78%	1.5	1.2	79%
Malta, Gibraltar, Cyprus	0.4	0.5		0.5	0.9	
Other	3.3	3.1	79%	3.3	2.8	80%
No. of births	722,961*	1,998	87%	688,989*	1,995	87%

* Information was not available about the place of birth of 0.3% of
  mothers, 5.0% of fathers. These have been excluded.

Social class

The response rate was slightly higher among the middle class, 90%,
than among the working class, 86%. The apparently poor response
among the Armed Forces, 72%, may be the result of their mobility
but it may be that the coding was not entirely consistent.   Sometimes the occupation if it was known may have been coded and sometimes it may just have been classified as 'Armed Forces'.

Study areas

In the 25 different study areas the response rate ranged from 96%

to 78%.   It was 88% in rural districts against 86% in other areas -
a difference which might have occurred by chance.   The variation in
different regions is shown in Table C.

TABLE C   Response rate in regions

Region	Study areas	Proportion interviewed	No. in group (=100%)
London	Barking, L.B., Enfield L.B., Islington L.B., Southwark L.B.	82%	320
Elsewhere in the South	Slough (Bucks), Andover (Hants), Rochester (Kent), Walton and Weybridge (Surrey), Plymouth (Devon), Bath (Somerset)	89%	480
Midlands and Wales	East Dereham (Norfolk), Birmingham, Leamington Spa (Warwickshire), Stoke-on-Trent (Staffs), Buxton (Derbys), Wellingborough (Northampton), Horwich (Lancs), Llantrisant (Glam), Clowne (Derbys)	88%	720
North	Tadcaster (W.Yorks), Maryport (Cumberland), Hull (E.Yorks), Sheffield (W.Yorks), Berwick-on-Tweed (Northumberland), Oldham (Lancs)	87%	480
All regions		87%	2,000

The response in London was appreciably lower than elsewhere but
there was no significant difference between the other regions.
This means that in the initial sample 16% of the births were in
London;   among the successful interviews this proportion was 15%.

Length of marriage and age of parents

Since these two characteristics are closely related they are
considered together.   The national figures for length of marriage
relate only to women married once only, so 3.1% of legitimate live
births are excluded.   Table D shows that the final sample of
parents interviewed had rather fewer births to mothers of 35 or
more than might be expected from the 1972 national figures.   This
may be because older mothers and fathers were less willing to take
part in the study, or because there was some bias in the initial
sample.

TABLE D Length of marriage and age of mother

	Legitimate births 1972	Successful interviews
Length of marriage at time of birth of baby (completed years):	%	%
0	13.6	14.2
1	12.0	13.4
2	13.3	15.1
3	13.0	10.5
4	11.0	10.1
5 - 9	26.5	26.7
10 - 14	7.5 ⎤	7.3 ⎤
15 - 19	2.5 ⎬ 10.6	1.7 ⎬ 10.0
20 or more	0.6 ⎦	1.0 ⎦
Number of births	642,305*	1,728
Age of mother:	%	%
Under 20	8.7	9.7
20 - 24	34.6	37.5
25 - 29	35.6	33.8
30 - 34	14.0	13.6
35 - 39	5.6 ⎤	4.6 ⎤
40 or more	1.5 ⎦ 7.1	0.8 ⎦ 5.4
Number of births	662,929	1,724

* To women married once only.

In addition, there were more births to fathers under 20, 3.5% compared with 2.6%.

Number of previous liveborn children

There was some indication of a smaller proportion of high parity births to mothers in the sample compared with all legitimate births in 1972 (see Table E).   But these differences might have occured by chance.

TABLE E Number of previous liveborn children to mothers

	Legitimate births 1972	Successful interviews with mothers
	%	%
0	40.8	41.8
1	34.8	34.2
2	14.6	15.1
3	5.7	5.2
4	2.2	2.4
5 or more	1.9	1.3
Number of mothers (= 100%)	642,305*	1,473

* To women married once only

Premarital conceptions

This was calculated for all first births.   It was 24.9% for the
study births compared with 22.7% for legitimate first births in
1972 - a difference which might well occur by chance.

COMPARISON OF SOME FACTUAL DATA FROM MOTHERS AND FATHERS

The decision about which parent should be interviewed was made at
random.   There should therefore be no difference between the samples
of mothers and fathers in the data recorded on the birth certificates
- or in the factual data reported at interview although some
variations might arise in the latter because of the somewhat lower
response rate among fathers.
    No differences were observed in the characteristics recorded on
the birth certificate, but more of the fathers interviewed than of
the mothers said they owned their present home - 58% compared with
49%.   In addition, fathers reported a slightly lower average number
of children for the couple than did mothers - 1.80 against 1.96.
(The definition was all natural children of either the mother or
father who were now living with them or away temporarily and any of
both mother and father who had grown up and left home.   Children
adopted by the couple were included but not those who were fostered.)
Fathers also reported a slightly lower average household size - 4.0
people compared with 4.2 - but there was no difference in the
proportions saying they lived in households of a primary family unit
of parents and children only.   Nor were there any differences in
their reports on length of marriage or the mother's age at first
pregnancy.
    There was no difference between the samples of mothers and fathers
in their reports on whether they or their spouses left school as soon
as it was possible to do so, but whereas 62% of the fathers said they
had had some further education, only 53% of the mothers said their
husbands fell into that category.   And whereas 14% of the fathers
said they had no religion, only 8% of mothers said this about their
husbands.   There was no difference in the proportions reported to
be Catholics.

THE MOVERS

Forty-four of the parents who were successfully interviewed, 2.5%,
had moved outside the study area but their new addresses were traced
and they were followed up and seen.   A further 140, 8.1%, had
moved within the same area.   In addition 1% of the initial sample
were not seen because they had left England and Wales and 1.5%
could not be traced.   In the earlier study, 'Parents and Family
Planning Services', no attempt was made to follow up people who had
moved out of the area and 9.8% were excluded for that reason.   (This
was because that survey was concerned with relating parents'
experiences to the birth control services available within the area.
Information was collected about services in the study areas.)   It
seems likely that a number of those classified on the present survey

as moving within the same area had in fact moved outside it but were
still near enough to be contacted by the same interviewer - and it
was the administrative procedure of passing the address on to another
interviewer which determined the classification rather than movement
over the local authority boundary.   This, together with the fact
that those who had moved within the study area were not identified
in the earlier inquiry, makes it difficult to estimate the effect of
trying to include all movers within England and Wales.   But it seems
likely that this policy helped to increase the response rate.
Taking the initial sample selected as the base, 87% were successfully
interviewed on the present survey compared with 81% in the earlier
one.

To see whether the inclusion of the movers is likely to affect
comparisons between the two studies, some of the characteristics of
those who moved both within and outside the study area were examined.

A wide range of variables was considered.   Aspects of fertility
behaviour such as current contraceptive use, mother's age at first
pregnancy, length of marriage, number of children already born and
number wanted altogether did not differ significantly between the
movers and non-movers.   Nor did such social characteristics as
education, religion, place of birth and social class.

It seemed more likely that housing circumstances might differ
between those who had moved recently and those who had not done so.
In fact, household composition, household amenities and the number
of persons per room did not vary significantly and the only difference that emerged was in the nature of their accommodation.   Those
now living in Council houses or flats and those privately renting
unfurnished accommodation were less likely to have moved outside
the initial study area than those living in other types of accommodation (1% compared with 3%).   Those living in privately rented
furnished accommodation were the most likely to have moved at all -
24% against 10%.

These differences probably arise because of the insecurity and
unsatisfactory nature of much of the furnished accommodation and the
difficulty of obtaining unfurnished accommodation to rent either
from Councils or privately.

However, the differences do not seem large enough to affect
comparisons between the present study and 'Parents and Family
Planning Services'.

CLASSIFICATION OF SOCIAL CLASS

As our index of social class we took the father's occupation and classified it according to the Registrar General's Classifications of Occupations (Office of Population Censuses and Surveys, 1970). This distinguishes six 'social class' groups:

    I   Professional, etc. occupations
    II   Intermediate occupations
   III Skilled occupations
         (N) non-manual
         (M) manual
   IV Partly skilled occupations
    V   Unskilled occupations

These classes are intended to reflect 'the general standing within the community of the occupations concerned'. In a number of instances the main differences that emerge are between what can be described as the 'middle class' and 'working class', the former being most of the non-manual occupations - the Registrar General's social classes I, II and III non-manual - and the latter almost entirely manual - III manual, IV and V.

Data about this were obtained from two sources, the birth certificates and the interviews. They were both coded, independently, at the Institute for Social Studies in Medical Care. The distributions are compared in Table F.

A relatively small proportion of occupations recorded at the interview were classified as unskilled, 5% compared with 8% of those on the birth certificates. This happened for both mothers and fathers. There was no significant difference between the distributions for mothers and fathers.

A cross analysis of data from the birth certificates and the interviews with mothers showed that 75% of the occupations were in precisely the same category, 15% differed by one category and 10% by more than one. Proportions for the data from fathers were similar: 76%, 16% and 8%. So it did not appear that information from the fathers about their own occupations was more accurate or consistent. And of course the information from the birth certificates and the interviews related to different points in time and there may have been some genuine changes.

TABLE F Social class distributions based on data from two different sources.

	Mothers		Fathers		Mothers and fathers	
	Birth certificate	Interviews	Birth certificate	Interviews	Birth certificate	Interviews
	%	%	%	%	%	%
I Professional	7	6	5	7	6	7
II Intermediate	14	16	15	13	14	15
III Skilled non-manual	9	10	12	8	10	9
Skilled manual	44	45	44	51	44	46
IV Partly-skilled	18	18	16	16	18	18
V Unskilled	8	5	8	5	8	5
Number classified (= 100%)	1,406	1,418	254	256	1,660	1,674
Proportion not classified	5%	4%	3%	3%	4%	4%

Analysis by the number of different jobs the father had had from the time one year before his marriage showed that agreement between the birth certificate and interview data was greatest, 81%, for those with one job declining to 72% of those who had had two or more.

Data from the birth certificates have generally been used in the report as these were available even when the mothers were not interviewed.   This was also done in 'Parents and Family Planning Services'.

Appendix III

STATISTICAL SIGNIFICANCE AND SAMPLING ERRORS

There are a number of factors, particularly the nature of the data and the stage at which precise hypotheses were often formulated, which violate some of the conditions in which statistical tests of significance apply and make interpretation difficult.   For this reason they are rarely referred to in the text, in an attempt to avoid the appearance of spurious precision which the presentation of such tests might seem to imply.   But in the absence of more satisfactory techniques these tests have been used to give some indication of the probability of differences occurring by chance.

Chi-square, t, chi-square trend tests and tests for differences between proportions have been applied constantly when looking at the data from this survey and have influenced decisions about what differences to present and how much verbal 'weight' to attach to them.   In general, attention has not been drawn to any difference which statistical tests suggest might have occurred by chance five or more times in 100.

Another difficulty about presenting results from a study like this with over 250 items of basic information is that of selection. Inevitably not all cross-analyses are carried out - only about 1,450 - and only a fraction of these are presented, which of course gives rise to difficulty in interpreting significance.   Positive results are more often shown than negative ones.   Readers may sometimes wonder why certain further analyses are not reported. Often, but not always, the analysis will have been done but the result found to be negative or inconclusive.

Table G shows the sampling error for a number of characteristics. (For appropriate formula see Gray and Corlett, 1950.)   Because of the wide variations between areas the design effect is greater than two for the proportion of mothers who had consulted a doctor at a family planning clinic and for the proportion reporting ownership of a house.

The position is summarized in Table H which shows the family size distribution of first the sample at the time of interview, then the final family size of the sample, and of the population from which it was drawn.

TABLE G Sampling errors

	Value in total sample	Range in 25 study areas	Sampling error	Estimated random sampling error*	Range ± two sampling errors	Design effect**
Proportion of mothers who had consulted a doctor at a family planning clinic	29.3%	1.8%-54.0%	2.5%	1.2%	24.3%-34.3%	2.1
Proportion of mothers now taking the pill	42.6%	26.1%-59.0%	2.0%	1.3%	38.6%-46.6%	1.5
Proportion of mothers reporting current use of withdrawal	6.3%	0.0%-20.0%	1.0%	0.6%	4.3%- 8.3%	1.7
Proportion of mothers wanting more children	43.9%	29.0%-58.3%	1.3%	1.3%	41.3%-46.5%	1.0
Proportion of mothers aged less than 20 at first pregnancy	24.2%	10.5%-35.5%	1.4%	1.1%	21.4%-27.0%	1.3
Proportion of mothers reporting ownership of house, with mortgage	43.8%	9.6%-76.7%	3.2%	1.3%	37.4%-50.2%	2.5

* If a random sample of country, that is $\sqrt{\dfrac{p.q}{n}}$

** The ratio of the sampling error with the given two-stage sample design to the estimated random sampling error.

TABLE H Distribution of family size in sample and in population
from which selected

| Number of children in family | Sample as selected | Final family size of | |
		Sample	Population from which drawn
	%	%	%
1	41.6	7.3	17.5
2	34.3	38.4	46.2
3	15.1	29.7	23.8
4	5.2	10.8	6.5
5	2.5	6.0	2.9
6 or more	1.3	7.8	3.1
	100.0	100.0	100.0
Average	1.96	2.93	2.40

How does this bias affect the estimates of the proportion with a
particular family size at the time of interview who will have
another? It is possible to compare from the figures in Table H the
proportions who will have another child from the sample as selected
and from the population from which it was drawn.

In the population, 82.5% of those with one child will have a
second.   The estimate of this that would be made from the sample
as selected is that $\frac{34.3}{41.6}$ = 82.5% would do so.   Similarly in the
population $\frac{36.3}{82.5}$ = 44.0% of those with two children will have a
third, while the estimate of this from the sample would be $\frac{15.1}{34.3}$
= 44.0%.   The sample is biased in its distribution of family size
but within each family size there is no bias.

The bias is important in terms of the use of contraception as
the sample is obviously biased towards the ineffective contracep-
tors - those who have an additional baby 'by mistake' have an
additional chance of being included in the sample, those who do not
make such a mistake will not have this extra chance.   This means
that factors related to the achievement or failure of intentions
will have a biased distribution in the sample.

FAMILY SIZE AND THE BIAS IN THE SAMPLE

As explained in the Introduction, by taking a sample of births the sample is biased towards parents who will eventually have relatively large families.   This was illustrated by taking the family size distribution of the sample at the time of interview and calculating the average final family size of the sample and of the population from which it was drawn on the obviously unrealistic assumption that fertility remains constant over time.   The details of that calculation are given here.

The distribution of the sample's family size at the time of interview was:-

Number of children in family at interview	%
1	41.6
2	34.3
3	15.1
4	5.2
5	2.5
6 or more	1.3

Those who had six children at the time of interview must at some stage have had five children and at an earlier stage four etc. It is also obvious that some of those with a given number of children will go on to have another child whereas some will stop at the number they already have.   On the assumption of constant fertility it is clear that the 2.5% who have five children is made up of 1.3% who will have another and therefore 1.2% will stick at five. Similarly of those with four 1.3% will go on and have six or more, 1.2% will have five and therefore 2.7% will stick at four.   The distribution for all the family sizes is shown in Table I.

The average family size at the time of interview was 1.96 children (this is calculated from the raw data; calculated from the percentages it would be 1.97) whereas the final family size of the sample would be 2.93.

But since the basis of the sample was children not families, those families who would have six children could be included after their first, second, third, fourth, fifth or sixth child whereas those who

would have one could only be included after the birth of that one
child.   To calculate the final family size of the population
from which the sample was drawn the proportions have to be reweighted
by the number of children in the family.   This is done in Table J.

TABLE I Distribution of family size of sample at interview and when completed

Number of children	Number of children						Final family size %
	1	2	3	4	5	6+	
1	7.3						7.3
2	19.2	19.2					38.4
3	9.9	9.9	9.9				29.7
4	2.7	2.7	2.7	2.7			10.8
5	1.2	1.2	1.2	1.2	1.2		6.0
6	1.3	1.3	1.3	1.3	1.3	1.3	7.8
Family size at interview	41.6	34.3	15.1	5.2	2.5	1.3	100.0

TABLE J Distribution of final family size of sample and the population from which it was drawn

Number of children in family	Final family size of sample %	Reweighted proportions	Reweighted percentage
1	7.3	7.3	17.5
2	38.4	19.2	46.2
3	29.7	9.9	23.8
4	10.8	2.7	6.5
5	6.0	1.2	2.9
6	7.8	1.3	3.1
	100.0	41.6	100.0

BIBLIOGRAPHY

ÁSKHAM, JANET (1975), 'Fertility and Deprivation: A study of differential fertility amongst working-class families in Aberdeen', Cambridge University Press.

BLAKE, JUDITH (1968), Are babies consumer durables? A critique of the economic theory of reproductive motivation, 'Population Studies', vol.22, pp.5-25.

BONE, MARGARET (1973), 'Family Planning Services in England and Wales', London, HMSO.

BOTT, ELIZABETH (1957), 'Family and Social Network', London, Tavistock Publications.

BUSFIELD, JOAN (1974), Ideologies and reproduction, in M.P.M. Richards, 'The Integration of the Child into a Social World', Cambridge University Press.

CARTWRIGHT, ANN and TUCKER, WYN (1969), An experiment with an advance letter on an interview inquiry, 'British Journal of Preventive and Social Medicine', vol.23, pp.241-3.

CARTWRIGHT, ANN (1970), 'Parents and Family Planning Services', London, Routledge & Kegan Paul.

CARTWRIGHT, ANN and WAITE, MARJORIE (1972), General practitioners and contraception in 1970-71, 'Journal of the Royal College of General Practitioners', supplement no.2, vol.22.

CARTWRIGHT, ANN and LUCAS, SUSAN (1974), Survey of abortion patients for the Committee on the working of the Abortion Act, 'Report of the Committee on the working of the Abortion Act', vol.3, London, HMSO.

CARTWRIGHT, ANN and MOFFETT, JOANNA (1974), A comparison of results obtained by men and women interviewers in a fertility survey, 'Journal of Biosocial Science', vol.6, pp.315-22.

CARTWRIGHT, ANN and PRINCE, ELIZABETH (1975), The repeatability of data obtained in a fertility survey, 'Journal of Biosocial Science', vol.7, pp.207-31.

CENTRAL STATISTICAL OFFICE (1974), 'Social Trends', no.5, London, HMSO.

COHEN, ALBERT K. and HODGES, HAROLD M. Jr. (1963), Characteristics of the lower-blue-collar-class, 'Social Problems', vol.10, no.4, pp.303-34.

DUNNELL, KAREN and CARTWRIGHT, ANN (1972), 'Medicine Takers, Prescribers and Hoarders', London, Routledge & Kegan Paul.

188

FARID, S.M. (1974), 'The Current Tempo of Fertility in England and Wales', Medical and Population Studies no.27, London, HMSO.

FARID, S.M., forthcoming publication on generation fertility. London, HMSO.

FREEDMAN, D. (1963), The relation of economic status to fertility, 'American Economic Review', vol.53(I), pp.414-26.

FREEDMAN, RONALD, WHELPTON, PASKAL K. and CAMPBELL, ARTHUR A. (1959), 'Family Planning, Sterility and Population growth', McGraw Hill.

FREEDMAN, RONALD and COOMBS, LOLAGENE (1966), Economic considerations in family growth decisions, 'Population Studies', vol.20, pp.197-222.

GENERAL REGISTER OFFICE (1960), 'The Registrar-General's Statistical Review of England and Wales for the Year 1959', part II, London, HMSO.

GENERAL REGISTER OFFICE (1966), 'Census 1961 England and Wales: Fertility Tables', London, HMSO.

GENERAL REGISTER OFFICE (1966), 'The Registrar-General's Statistical Review of England and Wales for the Year 1964', part II, London HMSO.

GENERAL REGISTER OFFICE (1970), 'The Registrar-General's Statistical Review of England and Wales for the Year 1968', part II, London, HMSO.

GENERAL REGISTER OFFICE (1972), 'The Official List for 1972', part I, London, HMSO.

GORER, GEOFFREY (1971), 'Sex and Marriage in England today. A study of the views and experience of the under-45s', Nelson.

GRAY, P.G. and CORLETT, T. (1950), Sampling for the Social Survey, 'Journal of the Royal Statistical Society', Series A, vol.113, part II, pp.150-99.

HARRIS, C.C. (1969), 'The Family', London, George Allen & Unwin.

HAWTHORN, GEOFFREY (1970), 'The Sociology of Fertility: Themes and issues in modern sociology', London, Collier-Macmillan.

HAWTHORN, GEOFFREY (1974), The birth rate, and what lies behind it, 'New Society', 4 July, pp.8-11.

ILLICH, IVAN (1975), 'Medical Nemesis: the expropriation of health', London, Calder & Boyars.

INEICHEN, BERNARD and HOOPER, DOUGLAS (1974), Wives' mental health and children's behaviour problems in contrasting residential areas, 'Social Science and Medicine', vol.8, pp.369-74.

JAMES, W.H. (1971), The reliability of the reporting of coital frequency, 'Journal of Sex Research', vol.7, p.312.

JEPHCOTT, PEARL (1971), 'Homes in High Flats: some of the human problems involved in multi-storey housing', Edinburgh, Oliver & Boyd.

'LANCET' (1974), 'The pill off prescription?', vol.2, pp.933-4.

LANGFORD, CHRISTOPHER, 'Fertility and Contraceptive Practice in Britain: a report on a survey carried out in 1967/68', Forthcoming.

LEIBENSTEIN, HARVEY (1975), The economic theory of fertility decline, 'Quarterly Journal of Economics', vol.89, no.1.

LEPPO, KIMMO, KOSKELAINEN, OSMO and SIEVERS, KAI (1973-4), Contraceptive practices in Finland in 1971, 'Yearbook of Population Research in Finland', vol.13, pp.47-60, Helsinki, Population Research Institute (Vaestontutkimuslaitos).

McEWAN, J.A., OWENS, CAROL and NEWTON, J.R. (1974), Pregnancy in girls under 17: a preliminary study in a hospital district in South London, 'Journal of Biosocial Science', vol.6, pp.357-81.

MITTON, ROGER (1973), Family planning clinics in 1970, 'Family Planning', July, pp.30-2.

MOSER, C.A. (1972), Statistics about immigrants: objectives, sources, methods and problems, 'Social Trends', no.3, pp.20-30.
'NEW SOCIETY' (1975), Hiding in figs, 9 January, p.52.
OFFICE OF POPULATION CENSUSES AND SURVEYS (1970), 'Classification of Occupations 1970', London, HMSO.
OFFICE OF POPULATION CENSUSES AND SURVEYS (1970), 'The Registrar-General's Statistical Review of England and Wales for the Year 1968', Supplement on Abortion, London, HMSO.
OFFICE OF POPULATION CENSUSES AND SURVEYS (1971), 'The Registrar-General's Statistical Review of England and Wales for the Year 1969', part II, London, HMSO.
OFFICE OF POPULATION CENSUSES AND SURVEYS (1971), 'The Registrar-General's Statistical Review of England and Wales for the Year 1969', Supplement on Abortion, London, HMSO.
OFFICE OF POPULATION CENSUSES AND SURVEYS (1972a), 'The Registrar-General's Statistical Review of England and Wales for the Year 1970', part II, London, HMSO.
OFFICE OF POPULATION CENSUSES AND SURVEYS (1972b), 'The Registrar-General's Statistical Review of England and Wales for the Year 1970', Supplement on Abortion, London, HMSO.
OFFICE OF POPULATION CENSUSES AND SURVEYS (1972c), 'Population Projections', no.2 1971-2011, London, HMSO.
OFFICE OF POPULATION CENSUSES AND SURVEYS (1973), 'The Registrar-General's Statistical Review of England and Wales for the Year 1971', part II, London, HMSO.
OFFICE OF POPULATION CENSUSES AND SURVEYS (1973), 'The Registrar-General's Statistical Review of England and Wales for the Year 1971', Supplement on Abortion, London, HMSO.
OFFICE OF POPULATION CENSUSES AND SURVEYS (1974a), 'The Registrar-General's Statistical Review of England and Wales for the Year 1972', part II, London, HMSO.
OFFICE OF POPULATION CENSUSES AND SURVEYS (1974b), 'The Registrar-General's Statistical Review of England and Wales for the Year 1972', Supplement on Abortion, London, HMSO.
OFFICE OF POPULATION CENSUSES AND SURVEYS (1974c), 'The Registrar-General's Statistical Review of England and Wales for the Year 1973', Supplement on Abortion, London, HMSO.
OFFICE OF POPULATION CENSUSES AND SURVEYS (1974d), 'The Registrar-General's Quarterly Return for England and Wales', no.502, 2nd quarter 1974, London, HMSO.
OFFICE OF POPULATION CENSUSES AND SURVEYS (1975), 'The Registrar-General's Statistical Review of England and Wales for the Year 1973', part II, London, HMSO.
PLATT, JENNIFER (1969), Some problems in measuring the jointness of conjugal role-relationships, 'Sociology', vol.3, pp.287-97.
PEEL, JOHN (1970), The Hull Family Survey 1, The survey couples, 1966, 'Journal of Biosocial Science', vol.2, pp.45-70.
PEEL, JOHN and CARR, GRISELDA (1975), 'Contraception and Family Design. A study of birth planning in contemporary society', Edinburgh, London and New York, Churchill Livingstone.
RAINWATER, LEE (1960), 'And the Poor Get Children', Chicago, Quadrangle Books.
RAINWATER, LEE (1965), 'Family Design: marital sexuality, family size and contraception', Chicago, Aldine.

ROYAL COLLEGE OF GENERAL PRACTITIONERS (1974), 'Oral Contraceptives and Health: An interim report from the Oral Contraception Study of the Royal College of General Practitioners', Pitman Medical.
RYDER, NORMAN B. and WESTOFF, CHARLES F. (1971), 'Reproduction in the United States 1965', Princeton University Press.
SCHNEIDERMAN, LEONARD (1964), Value orientation preferences of chronic relief recipients, 'Social Work', vol.9, no.3, pp.13-18.
SCOWEN, E.F. (1969), Oral contraceptives containing oestrogens, 'Lancet', vol.2, p.1369.
SMITH, GILLIAN CRAMPTON (1973), 'Too Great a Risk!', London, Family Planning Association (S.W. London Branch).
SMITH, GILLIAN CRAMPTON (1975), 'Don't Rush Me!', London, Wandsworth Council for Community Relations.
TURNER, CHRISTOPHER (1967), Conjugal roles and social networks: a re-examination of an hypothesis, 'Human Relations', vol.20, pp.121-30.
WESTOFF, CHARLES F., POTTER, ROBERT G. Jr, SAGI, PHILIP C. and MISHLER, ELLIOT G. (1961), 'Family Growth in Metropolitan America', Princeton University Press.
WESTOFF, CHARLES F., POTTER, ROBERT G. Jr and SAGI, PHILIP C. (1963), 'The Third Child: A study in the prediction of fertility',Princeton University Press.
WESTOFF, CHARLES F. (1974), Coital frequency and contraception, 'Family Planning Perspectives', vol.6, pp.136-41.
WHELPTON, PASCAL K., CAMPBELL, ARTHUR A. and PATTERSON, JOHN E. (1966), 'Fertility and Family Planning in the United States', Princeton University Press.
WILLMOTT, PETER and YOUNG, MICHAEL (1960), 'Family and Class in a London Suburb', London, Routledge & Kegan Paul.
WOOLF, MYRA (1971), 'Family Intentions', London, HMSO.
YOUNG, MICHAEL and WILLMOTT, PETER (1957), 'Family and Kinship in East London', London, Routledge & Kegan Paul.

INDEX

abortion
> and the birth rate, 11, 18
> attitudes to, 67-72, 168
> rates in England and Wales, 8, 10, 41

Abortion Act, 8
Abortion (Amendment) Bill, 170
abstinence, 52
age
> of babies at time of interview, 5
> of fathers, 103, 110, 160, 177
> of mothers at birth of study baby, 176, 177; and attitudes to abortion, 68, 70; and contact with own mother, 149; and contraception, 49-50, 51, 54; and discussion of birth control, 79, 80; and family size, 148; and frequency of intercourse, 88-9; and home ownership, 115; and hopes for further children, 17, 18, 95, 96; and marital relationship, 157, 160-1; and person felt closest to, 150; and pill, 61, 108; and social class, 103; and sterilization, 63, 64, 67; and sub-fertility, 86-7; and time taken to conceive, 91
> of mothers at first pregnancy, 178, 179; and family size, 41; and mother's intentions, 35; and place of birth, 140; and size of family of origin, 145, 146, 151; and social class, 103-4, 113

of mothers at marriage, 7, 9, 170; and family size, 112; and social class, 103-4, 113; and timing of first birth, 34, 37
agnostics, see non-believers
amenities, see housing, conditions
Andover, study area, 174, 176
Armed Forces, 176
Askham, Janet, 107, 113, 120, 167
atheist, see non-believers

Barking, study area, 174, 176
Bath, study area, 174, 176
Belford, 173, 176
Berwick-upon-Tweed, 3, 173, 176
Bethnal Green, 151
Birmingham, study area, 3, 173, 176
birth control, 11, 16, 18, 40, 45-56, 168
> changes in use of: 12-14; in the future, 53-6, 57
> discussion of, 73-83, 142-3, 155-64
> fathers: attitudes to, 153, 154; use of, 13-14
> medical appropriation of, 168-9
> mothers: attitudes to different methods, 57-67, 71-2, 80; use of, 12-14 - and contact with own mother, 150; and place of birth, 140-2, 150-1; and unemployment, 137; and views on likelihood of becoming pregnant, 46-8; and

tions, 170; and social class, 111-12, 181; views and family size intentions, 96-8, 134-6
Workington, see Maryport and Workington
World Health Organization, 122
World Population Year, 122, 126

Yorkshire East Riding, study area in, see Kingston-upon-Hull
Yorkshire West Riding, study areas in, see Sheffield and Tadcaster
Young, Michael, 148, 151, 168